Sober and Still Sharp

Recovery for High-Performing Professionals

Nicci Brochard
&
Dr. Ben Chuba

Sober and Still Sharp

Recovery for High-Performing Professionals

CROSSBORDER

New York, London, Quebec

Contents

Introduction: The Mask of Success

In today's achievement-driven world, the image of the high-performing professional is often one of confidence, control, and success. These individuals are often seen as the epitome of accomplishment—climbing the corporate ladder, leading teams, securing deals, and excelling in their fields. From the outside, they appear invincible, driven, and fully in control. However, beneath the polished exterior lies a silent crisis—high-functioning addiction.

High-functioning addiction is a phenomenon where individuals successfully navigate their personal and professional lives while secretly battling substance abuse or compulsive behaviors. These professionals manage to maintain outward appearances of success, often masking their internal struggles with a façade of competence and control. They show up at work, meet deadlines, and appear to be on top of their game, all while battling a hidden addiction that threatens their physical, mental, and emotional well-being. The very traits that make them successful—drive, ambition, and a relentless work ethic—can also fuel their destructive behaviors.

For many high-functioning professionals, addiction is not something that fits the typical mold of a "substance abuser." They don't fit the image of someone struggling on the streets or in a rehab facility. Instead, they are in positions of influence, leadership, and respect. They have perfected the art of maintaining the illusion of success while quietly grappling with a deep, internal struggle. This is the paradox of high-functioning addiction—success on the outside, but inner turmoil that threatens to derail everything.

The Unique Psychology of High-Performing Professionals

High-performing professionals tend to possess a unique set of psychological traits that both contribute to their success and, paradoxically, enable their addiction to thrive. These individuals are typically ambitious, competitive, driven by perfectionism, and often possess an insatiable need for validation. They are accustomed to functioning under high levels of stress and pressure, often pushing themselves to the brink of burnout in order to achieve their goals. For them, success is not just about external accomplishments; it's about proving their worth, not only to others but also to themselves.

This relentless drive for excellence can create a perfect storm for addiction. The pressures of maintaining high standards, the constant pursuit of more, and the need to suppress vulnerabilities can lead these professionals to seek solace in substances or unhealthy behaviors. What begins as a way to cope with stress, enhance performance, or temporarily escape becomes a hidden dependency that only worsens over time. For many, their addiction is not a conscious decision; it's a reaction to the overwhelming pressures of their world.

High-performing professionals also tend to be overachievers, often pushing themselves to prove their worth, especially in highly competitive industries. This relentless drive for achievement becomes part of their identity. The problem arises when the addiction begins to take hold, and their need for success becomes intertwined with their need for the substance or behavior they rely on. Their ability to compartmentalize allows them to keep functioning at high levels while the addiction silently escalates. However, the cost to their mental, emotional, and physical health is significant and often masked by their ability to perform in the workplace.

The Silent Crisis: Addiction Masked by Achievement

The most insidious aspect of high-functioning addiction is its ability to remain hidden. On the surface, these individuals are often the epitome of success. They are the CEOs, the partners, the top performers in their industries. They meet deadlines, attend meetings, and show up in all the right places. From the outside, everything seems to be in order—except for the silent crisis happening beneath the surface. Their addiction often goes unnoticed because their professional lives are so well-managed. The constant cycle of success and achievement allows them to maintain the illusion that everything is fine.

However, the internal toll is immense. High-functioning professionals often feel isolated in their struggle because they don't fit the typical image of an addict. They may not feel comfortable reaching out for help because they fear it will tarnish their professional reputation. The shame of having an addiction, particularly when it conflicts with their image as a high achiever, creates a barrier to seeking support. They may also feel that their addiction is justified by the stress and demands of their job—"I need this to keep going," or "Everyone else is doing it"—which allows them to justify their behavior for years, even as it begins to take a more significant toll on their health, relationships, and well-being.

The impact of this silent crisis can be devastating. Over time, the addiction begins to interfere with their performance, their relationships, and their ability to function in a healthy way. It erodes their sense of self, leaving them feeling increasingly trapped in a cycle of dependency, shame, and fear. They may experience episodes of burnout, emotional numbness, or anxiety, but these symptoms are often rationalized or dismissed as part of the pressures of the job. They may struggle with feelings of inadequacy, despite outward success, and may even experience a sense of imposter syndrome—feeling that they are not truly worthy of their accomplishments.

The key to addressing this crisis is understanding that success does not equal wellness. Just because someone is thriving professionally doesn't mean they are thriving personally. High-functioning addiction is a hidden epidemic among high-performing professionals, one that thrives on secrecy, shame, and silence.

Moving Forward

This book, *Sober and Still Sharp: Recovery for High-Performing Professionals*, seeks to provide a path forward for individuals caught in this silent crisis. It is designed to help high-performing professionals break the cycle of addiction while embracing recovery as a process of personal reinvention. By offering practical tools, strategies for reclaiming one's well-being, and personal stories of transformation, this book will guide readers in the process of healing and rebuilding their lives in a way that honors their quiet strength and resilience.

The journey to sobriety doesn't have to mean the end of ambition or the loss of your drive for excellence. In fact, recovery can be a reinvention of how you approach your work and your life. By understanding that true success is not about perfection or performance but about alignment with your values, wellness, and authenticity, you can break free from the grip of high-functioning addiction and thrive in ways that are more sustainable, fulfilling, and impactful than ever before.

In the following chapters, we will explore how to navigate this journey, redefine your success, and create a life that is sober, still sharp, and empowered. Through personal reflection, strategic recovery practices, and community support, we will dismantle the myth that success and addiction must go hand-in-hand, and instead embrace a future where wellness and achievement coexist.

Ben and I (Nicci) thank you immensely for choosing our book. We promise you will find in it what you are looking for.

Chapter 1

The Secret You Carry

Introduction

The world of high achievers often comes with a hidden side—one that remains veiled behind polished smiles, tailored suits, and well-crafted business cards. These individuals, who appear outwardly successful, are often carrying an unseen burden: addiction. Unlike the stereotypical image of addiction—a person on a street corner or in a dilapidated house—this addiction is neatly tucked behind the veneer of professional success. These are individuals who appear to have it all together, but underneath, they are grappling with substances or behaviors that are slowly, and sometimes silently, controlling their lives. The addiction may be hidden behind the briefcase, tucked behind the glass of a boardroom meeting, or hidden in the form of a workaholic's endless nights. This chapter delves into the secret addictions that many high-functioning, driven individuals struggle with, why they fall into such traps, and the substances and behaviors that fuel these hidden struggles.

Stories of Hidden Addiction Behind the Briefcase

John was the picture of success—a respected executive at a top multinational company, a father, and a husband. On the outside, he had everything that most people could wish for: a luxurious home, a beautiful family, a steady income, and a seemingly perfect life. However, few knew the real battle he was fighting. Every day, after dropping his children off at school and heading to the office, John's life spiraled into a world of alcohol consumption. The early morning meetings were followed by long hours at the bar, often with a client or a colleague. It wasn't about relaxation or unwinding—he used alcohol to numb the stress, anxiety, and fear of being exposed as a fraud. By evening, the carefully crafted exterior began to crumble, but only behind closed doors.

John was not alone. Many top-tier professionals and high-powered individuals secretly suffer from addiction while maintaining their outwardly perfect lives. Consider the case of Lisa, a lawyer at a prestigious law firm. By day, she was the epitome of professionalism—delivering court arguments with precision, leading her team, and dazzling clients with her intelligence. However, when the office doors closed, Lisa would retreat to her private space to gamble—an addiction she had developed during her college years but learned to hide. The secret gambling was her escape, her way of coping with the intense pressure of her profession. No one suspected a thing.

These stories aren't rare. They represent the hidden reality of many highly successful individuals. These professionals may not fit the traditional mold of an addict, yet their dependencies are just as real and, often, more destructive. The professional world can be demanding, and when someone is constantly expected to perform at high levels, the toll on their mental health can be significant. Instead of turning to a bottle of pills or a syringe, these individuals often find solace in what appear to be socially acceptable behaviors—behaviors that, when taken to an extreme, become their secret addictions.

Common Substances and Behaviors

While the nature of addiction may vary from one person to another, there are certain substances and behaviors that commonly lead individuals down the path of addiction, particularly among high-functioning professionals. These include alcohol, stimulants, workaholism, sex, and gambling. Let's examine each of these in more detail.

Alcohol

Alcohol is one of the most prevalent substances involved in addiction, especially among professionals. For many high-powered individuals, alcohol doesn't start as a problem. Initially, it's just a tool to celebrate success, bond with colleagues, or wind down after a stressful day. However, over time, alcohol can become a coping mechanism for dealing with stress, performance pressure, or even feelings of inadequacy.

Take the example of Mark, a senior executive at a tech company. Every business trip involved meeting clients over cocktails. While he started drinking in social settings, over time, the consumption became a routine that he couldn't break. For Mark, the glass of wine in the evening wasn't just about relaxation; it was about silencing the nagging voice of self-doubt that haunted him after each major deal. He didn't realize that his occasional drinking had escalated into a regular habit, one that started to negatively impact his work and relationships. In high-stakes professions, where the pressure to perform can be overwhelming, alcohol is often used to temporarily mute the noise of anxiety and uncertainty.

Stimulants

Stimulants—such as caffeine, nicotine, and more severe drugs like cocaine or methamphetamines—are another set of substances that high achievers frequently turn to. These substances are often used to increase energy levels, enhance focus, and prolong work hours. For the ambitious professional, stimulants can be seductive. They promise an ability to "do it all"—to handle multiple projects, to remain sharp during meetings, and to stay awake during late-night work sessions.

Take Sarah, a successful entrepreneur who built her startup from the ground up. She prided herself on her ability to juggle multiple tasks at once and keep up with the fast-paced demands of running her own business. However, as the pressure increased, so did her reliance on stimulants. Initially, she relied on coffee to get through long workdays, but eventually, she moved to more potent stimulants to maintain her energy. Soon, she found herself using substances to get through the day—caffeine in the morning, nicotine throughout the day, and a late-night dose of Adderall to push through the inevitable exhaustion. Her productivity skyrocketed, but so did her anxiety, insomnia, and physical health problems.

Workaholism

Workaholism, or the compulsive need to work long hours at the expense of personal well-being, is another form of addiction that is especially common among successful individuals. Unlike substance abuse, workaholism doesn't involve physical substances, but it can be just as damaging, especially in the long run. Workaholics tend to measure their self-worth by their output, often sacrificing relationships, health, and mental well-being in the process.

Consider the case of James, a successful corporate lawyer. His days were filled with client meetings, case preparations, and long hours at the office. When he wasn't working, he felt restless and anxious. To him, work was not just a job—it was a measure of his identity and success. His self-esteem was tied to his professional achievements. The need to be seen as constantly busy and indispensable to the firm drove him to ignore his personal life, health, and mental well-being. He spent his nights at the office, checking emails, and working on projects, unable to disconnect from the constant pressure to perform.

While many high achievers struggle with a strong work ethic, workaholism can be debilitating. The inability to switch off from work or take time for personal self-care can lead to burnout, emotional exhaustion, and strained relationships. Workaholics often find it difficult to relax because they associate their sense of worth with their productivity.

Sex Addiction

Sex addiction is another hidden form of addiction among professionals. Like many other forms of addiction, it often starts with the individual seeking an escape from stress, emotional distress, or a way to boost their self-esteem. For many professionals, sex addiction begins as a way to reaffirm their attractiveness, power, and success. They may use sex as a tool to feel desired or validated in their highly competitive professional environment. However, when these behaviors become compulsive and start to interfere with their personal and professional lives, they turn into an addiction.

Take the case of Robert, a high-level marketing executive. Robert was always the life of the party, known for his charm and confidence. He used his sex appeal to his advantage, leveraging relationships with clients and colleagues to climb the corporate ladder. However, his sexual exploits became a compulsion. What started as casual flings with clients and colleagues turned into a habit that drained him emotionally and physically. Robert was constantly seeking validation through sex, yet he found no lasting satisfaction. His addiction led to an affair that ultimately jeopardized both his career and personal life.

Gambling Addiction

Gambling is another form of addiction that is often hidden behind the façade of success. In high-pressure environments, individuals often turn to gambling as a form of escape or excitement. The rush of winning, even in small doses, can become a powerful way to cope with the stress and monotony of daily life.

David, an investment banker, found himself drawn to the excitement of high-stakes poker games. Initially, it was just a way to relax and unwind after a grueling week of work. However, over time, the stakes increased, and so did his dependency on gambling as a source of validation and thrill. He began using his success in business as a way to fund his gambling habit, thinking that he could always make more money to cover the losses. His addiction eventually led to financial instability, relationship issues, and a crumbling career.

Why Smart, Driven People Fall into Secret Addictions

It is often a perplexing question: why do intelligent, driven, and successful people fall into addiction? These are individuals who possess immense willpower, discipline, and ambition—qualities that seem to suggest they would be immune to the pull of addiction. However, addiction doesn't discriminate. It can strike even the most accomplished individuals, often because their intelligence and ambition make them more prone to certain behaviors.

One reason smart, driven people fall into secret addictions is that they often feel an intense pressure to perform. High achievers are constantly under the microscope, expected to deliver results, meet deadlines, and outdo themselves. This can create a constant cycle of stress and anxiety. In an attempt to cope with these pressures, many professionals turn to substances or behaviors that provide temporary relief or a sense of control. However, as the addiction deepens, the relief becomes fleeting, and the cycle continues.

Another reason is the fear of vulnerability. High-functioning individuals may feel that they cannot afford to show weakness or failure. Admitting to addiction may be seen as a sign of failure or incompetence, something that could threaten their career or reputation. As a result, they hide their struggles, believing that they can manage the addiction on their own without anyone knowing.

Finally, addiction often stems from a deep-seated emotional need for validation, success, or escape. Many high achievers struggle with perfectionism, constantly pushing themselves to meet unrealistic standards. When they fail to meet these standards, they may turn to substances or behaviors as a way to fill the emotional void or numb their feelings of inadequacy.

Conclusion

The hidden addictions carried behind the briefcase are a reality for many highly driven individuals. From alcohol to workaholism, sex addiction, gambling, and stimulants, these addictions can remain secret for years, often undetected by colleagues, friends, or even family. The reasons for these addictions are complex and multifaceted, often stemming from a combination of societal pressures, emotional needs, and a deep fear of vulnerability. It is essential for high achievers to recognize the potential risks of addiction and seek support when necessary to avoid falling further into destructive behaviors. The first step in breaking free from addiction is acknowledging its presence—only then can the path to healing and self-discovery begin.

Chapter 2

When Winning Is the Distraction

Introduction

Society places immense value on success, achievement, and productivity; the line between triumph and turmoil can often become dangerously thin. Success—while often celebrated as the pinnacle of one's ambitions—can inadvertently become both a distraction and a trap. It can serve as a shield that hides deeper emotional, mental, or physical struggles, masking the internal chaos behind a well-curated exterior of achievements and accolades. For many high performers, the pursuit of success becomes an insidious force that both protects them from vulnerability and enables their destructive behaviors. This chapter delves into how success can act as both armor and enabler, explores the psychological traps of perfectionism and imposter syndrome, and examines the myth of control that so often surrounds high achievers.

How Success Becomes Both Armor and Enabler

For many individuals, success is not merely a measure of accomplishment—it is a form of protection. When you succeed, you gain the respect and admiration of others. You gain resources, credibility, and influence. Success often shields you from criticism and shields you from the need to confront your inner struggles. It becomes your armor, allowing you to hide your vulnerabilities behind the accolades, the recognition, and the outward signs of achievement.

Take, for example, Richard, a young tech entrepreneur who built his startup into a multimillion-dollar company in less than five years. From the outside, Richard was the quintessential success story. His story was featured in top business magazines, his company received multiple rounds of venture capital funding, and his innovative product was hailed as revolutionary. Richard's success gave him the appearance of invulnerability—no one questioned him or doubted his abilities. However, beneath the success, Richard was struggling with anxiety, fear of failure, and an overwhelming need to maintain his high standards. He used work as his distraction, channeling every ounce of energy into growing his company to avoid confronting the personal demons that were creeping up behind the facade of triumph.

For Richard, and for many others, success can be both a crutch and a shield. It protects them from the need to address their inner conflicts, offering a constant source of validation that helps them to avoid self-reflection. At the same time, this relentless pursuit of success enables their addictions or unhealthy behaviors, whether that's substance use, workaholism, or even social withdrawal. The constant pursuit of winning creates a cycle—one that reinforces itself by continuously providing external affirmation, but without addressing the deeper issues that drive the need for such validation.

In fact, success can become an enabler of unhealthy patterns. When an individual achieves success, it often fuels the belief that more success will lead to more happiness or fulfillment. The cycle of achievement becomes self-reinforcing; the more one succeeds, the more one feels compelled to continue achieving. This cycle can lead to overwork, burnout, or the avoidance of personal challenges. Success becomes a carrot dangling just out of reach, and individuals find themselves chasing after it without ever truly feeling satisfied or fulfilled.

Perfectionism, Imposter Syndrome, and Relentless Productivity

One of the psychological traps that success often brings with it is perfectionism. Perfectionism is the belief that one must meet impossibly high standards and that anything less than flawless is unacceptable. It's a mindset that drives individuals to push themselves beyond their limits in the pursuit of excellence, but it also creates a cycle of chronic dissatisfaction. The pursuit of perfection, rather than bringing peace of mind or fulfillment, often leads to anxiety, exhaustion, and a feeling of never being "good enough."

Consider Clara, a senior project manager at a global consulting firm. Clara was known for her incredible attention to detail and her ability to deliver high-quality work under tight deadlines. To her colleagues, she was a model of productivity and effectiveness. However, behind closed doors, Clara's perfectionism was wreaking havoc on her mental health. She would spend hours reviewing reports, making sure that every number was accurate, every sentence perfectly worded. The slightest mistake, even if it went unnoticed by others, would send her into a spiral of self-criticism and shame. She felt that if she didn't meet the highest standards, she would lose her position or fail to live up to the expectations that others had of her.

Perfectionism, in many ways, feeds into the myth of control. If you can perfect everything around you, then surely you have control over your life, right? But this illusion of control can be a dangerous trap. Perfectionists often feel like they are juggling too many tasks, managing multiple projects, and meeting countless expectations, all while maintaining an outward image of flawless execution. They often find themselves working late into the night, sacrificing their personal time, relationships, and health in the name of excellence.

Imposter syndrome is another common phenomenon that often arises in high achievers who are struggling with perfectionism. Imposter syndrome is the persistent belief that one's success is undeserved, that they are merely "faking it" and will eventually be exposed as a fraud. This belief is particularly common among people who are highly driven and outwardly successful but who don't feel that they measure up internally.

Take the example of Michael, a software engineer at a top-tier company. Michael had been promoted to a senior role after just two years with the company, and his peers often praised his talent and expertise. Yet, no matter how much success he achieved, he never felt like he truly belonged. He constantly worried that one day, his colleagues or boss would realize that he wasn't as skilled as they thought. He felt as if he were playing a part, pretending to know everything while internally doubting his abilities. This fear of being exposed as an imposter led Michael to work harder, longer, and more obsessively than anyone else in his department. It was as though his worth depended on the next line of code he wrote, the next bug he fixed, or the next promotion he earned.

This cycle of perfectionism and imposter syndrome feeds into the notion that success can mask insecurity. The more driven a person becomes, the more likely they are to push themselves into a state of chronic productivity. Work becomes not just a means of success but a way to distract from feelings of inadequacy and self-doubt. It becomes a way to "prove" worth, both to others and to oneself. However, this constant need to be productive—without taking the necessary breaks to recharge or reflect—often leads to burnout and emotional exhaustion.

The Myth of "I've Got This Under Control"

One of the most dangerous beliefs that high achievers hold is the myth that they have everything "under control." This myth is a coping mechanism that allows individuals to maintain their image of competence and self-sufficiency. It allows them to ignore the signs of impending burnout, mental exhaustion, or emotional breakdown. This illusion of control is often reinforced by external validation—the praise of colleagues, the success of a project, the accolade of a promotion. In a world that celebrates achievement, it can be tempting to believe that success automatically equates to control.

Take Elizabeth, a marketing executive who had worked her way up the corporate ladder through sheer grit and determination. On the surface, she appeared to have it all together: a high-paying job, a supportive family, and a packed schedule full of meetings and events. However, inside, Elizabeth was drowning in stress. She would often cancel personal plans to stay late at work, promising herself that she would catch up later. Yet, the cycle never ended. Each day brought a new set of demands, and each night she went to bed feeling overwhelmed but unwilling to admit it to anyone—especially herself.

Elizabeth's belief that she had everything under control was, in fact, a defense mechanism. She was afraid that if she admitted she was struggling, it would mean she wasn't capable, wasn't as strong as she appeared to be. She avoided addressing her feelings of stress, anxiety, and exhaustion because it would force her to confront the possibility that her success was not sustainable or, worse, that she wasn't in control of her life at all. Instead of seeking help or finding ways to manage her workload, she pushed herself harder. The myth of control became her greatest distraction, leading her to a point where she couldn't distinguish between success and self-destruction.

The myth of control is particularly dangerous because it isolates the individual. It creates a false sense of independence, which discourages seeking help from others. When people believe they are "handling it all" on their own, they often distance themselves from their support networks, whether that's family, friends, or colleagues. They may even convince themselves that they don't need help or that asking for assistance would be a sign of weakness. As a result, they continue to push forward, becoming increasingly disconnected from their own needs and well-being.

Conclusion

Success, when viewed as the ultimate goal, can become both a distraction and a trap. For many high achievers, the pursuit of success acts as both armor and enabler, protecting them from confronting deeper issues and encouraging unhealthy patterns of perfectionism, imposter syndrome, and relentless productivity. The myth of control, which often accompanies this success, keeps them trapped in a cycle of striving and overwork, preventing them from acknowledging that they may not have it all under control. It's crucial for individuals to recognize that success alone is not a solution to life's challenges. In fact, it may be the very thing that prevents them from addressing the issues that matter most—their mental health, their relationships, and their overall well-being. Only when they acknowledge the distractions that success brings can they begin to forge a path toward true balance, self-awareness, and long-term fulfillment.

Chapter 3

Warning Signs You Ignore

Introduction

S uccess comes with its own set of pressures. High performers—whether entrepreneurs, executives, or creative professionals—often push themselves beyond the limits of ordinary effort, striving to exceed expectations, meet deadlines, and achieve greatness. While their outward achievements might be admired, they often ignore or overlook the warning signs that their mental, emotional, and physical well-being is declining. The warning signs of burnout, emotional distress, and physical deterioration often go unnoticed or are dismissed as part of the "price of success." This chapter explores how high performers disguise symptoms of dysfunction, the emotional and physical signs that often accompany the struggles they face, and the importance of recognizing these signs before they spiral into more serious consequences.

Functional vs. Dysfunctional: How High Performers Disguise Symptoms

The high-performing individual has a unique ability to mask dysfunction. The phrase "functional addict" might seem paradoxical, yet it accurately describes many people who manage to sustain outward success while quietly battling burnout, addiction, or mental health struggles. Functionality becomes a defense mechanism—a way to convince others and themselves that everything is under control, even when things are falling apart behind the scenes. These individuals are adept at compartmentalizing their problems, finding ways to continue achieving without allowing the visible signs of their inner turmoil to interfere with their work.

Take, for example, Anna, a top-level executive in a multinational company. She routinely worked 70-hour weeks, constantly juggling back-to-back meetings and overseeing several projects simultaneously. To her colleagues, Anna was a model of efficiency—smart, composed, and always delivering results. But Anna was hiding the emotional toll this lifestyle was taking on her. She was exhausted, anxious, and frequently overwhelmed, yet she could still perform at a high level. In fact, her success masked the early symptoms of burnout and mental exhaustion. Her ability to "get things done" allowed her to dismiss the toll it was taking on her mental health. She believed that as long as she continued delivering, there was no need to address her emotional and psychological well-being.

For high performers like Anna, it becomes easy to ignore the signs of dysfunction. Success allows them to push forward, and the external validation they receive provides enough motivation to maintain the illusion of control. But the more they ignore these signs, the more dysfunctional their behavior becomes. Eventually, this masking and compartmentalizing can lead to a tipping point—whether it manifests as a mental breakdown, physical collapse, or the unraveling of personal relationships.

Emotional Signs: Burnout, Numbness, Irritability

Emotional exhaustion is one of the most common and telling signs of dysfunction among high performers. The internal drive to succeed, combined with the external pressure to perform, often creates a perfect storm for emotional burnout. High achievers can fall into the trap of believing that their emotional state should be subordinated to their success. In doing so, they neglect or repress their emotional needs, leading to significant emotional signs that they may ignore or downplay.

Burnout

Burnout is perhaps the most well-known emotional symptom of excessive work and stress. It manifests as a state of complete physical, mental, and emotional exhaustion, where the individual feels that they are no longer able to continue functioning at a high level. For high performers, burnout often begins as a creeping feeling of fatigue. At first, they might simply feel tired after long workdays, but over time, this fatigue can grow to the point where it feels like an insurmountable weight.

Take the case of Thomas, an investment banker in a fast-paced, high-pressure environment. For years, Thomas had thrived under the stress of managing multimillion-dollar accounts and meeting ambitious targets. However, over time, the demands of his job began to take their toll. He found it harder to focus, his motivation waned, and he started to experience a sense of detachment from his work. What once excited him now felt like a burden, and he was unable to escape the constant feeling of being overwhelmed. Despite these warning signs, Thomas continued to push forward, believing that taking a break or acknowledging his exhaustion would be a sign of weakness. Eventually, this constant depletion led to a full-blown burnout, causing him to take an extended leave of absence.

Burnout is often characterized by a sense of hopelessness, a lack of energy, and an inability to feel joy or satisfaction from previously rewarding activities. For high performers, the emotional weight of burnout is compounded by the fear of falling behind or losing their edge. This fear drives them to keep going, further exacerbating their symptoms.

Numbness

Another emotional sign that high performers often ignore is emotional numbness. When the stress becomes too much to bear, the brain may attempt to shield itself from further harm by disconnecting from emotions. This numbness can feel like an emotional void, where the individual feels disconnected from themselves, their work, or their relationships. It is a form of emotional shutdown that allows the person to continue functioning, but at a much lower emotional capacity.

Consider the case of Ella, a creative director at an advertising agency. Ella was known for her innovative campaigns and her ability to push her team to achieve great results. However, as the demands of her role increased, so did the pressure to continuously produce. Over time, Ella began to feel increasingly numb. The excitement she once felt about her work had faded, and she started to feel disconnected from her team and her creative process. Although she continued to meet deadlines and lead her team effectively, she no longer felt passion or enthusiasm for her work. This numbness became a form of emotional survival—Ella could continue performing at a high level because her emotional engagement had been dulled. Yet, her lack of emotional connection to her work signaled a deeper issue that she chose to ignore.

Irritability

Irritability is another emotional sign that often accompanies burnout and emotional exhaustion. When the pressure to perform becomes too great, it can manifest as frustration, anger, or impatience with others. High performers often feel that they are carrying the weight of the world on their shoulders, and as a result, they may become short-tempered with colleagues, family members, or friends. This irritability is often a sign that the individual is emotionally drained and unable to manage the stress that is overwhelming them.

For example, Robert, a high-powered lawyer, would often snap at his colleagues over minor issues. What once would have been an easy conversation became a point of frustration and anger. His temper seemed to be growing shorter, and he became increasingly frustrated with the people around him. His colleagues began to notice the change in his demeanor, but Robert convinced himself that he was simply under pressure and that this was just part of the job. His irritability was a direct result of his inability to manage the emotional strain of his role, yet he chose to ignore it, believing that success and productivity would ultimately fix everything.

Physical Signs: Sleep Issues, Health Decline, Dependence

While emotional signs of dysfunction can be difficult to ignore, physical symptoms are often harder to hide. The body has a remarkable way of signaling distress, and high performers who push themselves to their limits will often experience physical signs of burnout, addiction, or mental strain. These signs are frequently dismissed as mere inconveniences or temporary issues, but they can be the body's way of sounding an alarm that cannot be ignored.

Sleep Issues

Sleep issues are one of the most common physical signs of dysfunction among high performers. Stress, anxiety, and the constant pressure to perform can disrupt sleep patterns, leading to insomnia, restless nights, and poor-quality rest. High achievers often prioritize work over sleep, convincing themselves that sleep deprivation is a necessary sacrifice in order to meet the demands of their roles. However, the long-term effects of chronic sleep deprivation can be catastrophic, leading to cognitive impairments, emotional instability, and a weakened immune system.

Take the example of Steven, a CEO of a rapidly growing tech company. Steven prided himself on working late into the night and getting up early to hit the ground running. He believed that sleep was overrated, and he could function on just a few hours of rest. However, over time, Steven began to notice that his concentration was slipping. He was forgetful, sluggish, and irritable during the day. His work performance suffered, and he started making mistakes that he would have never made in the past. Despite these signs, Steven continued to push himself, believing that he could "power through" and that sleep would come once he had completed the next task or milestone. His sleep deprivation was taking a significant toll on his physical and mental health, yet he chose to ignore it.

Health Decline

The physical toll of stress and overwork can also manifest in a decline in overall health. High performers often neglect their health, choosing to focus on work instead of exercise, proper nutrition, and self-care. The consequences of this neglect may not be immediately apparent, but over time, the lack of proper self-care can lead to weight gain, fatigue, digestive issues, or even more serious health conditions such as heart disease, high blood pressure, or diabetes.

For instance, Monica, a senior marketing executive, was constantly on the move. She skipped meals, worked through lunch, and rarely found time to exercise. Despite her success at work, her health began to deteriorate. She gained weight, felt fatigued all the time, and experienced digestive problems. She ignored the signs, thinking that as long as she continued to meet her professional goals, her health issues were just part of the deal. It wasn't until she collapsed from exhaustion during a business trip that she finally realized how much her neglect had cost her.

Dependence

Dependence—whether it be on caffeine, alcohol, prescription medication, or other substances—is another physical symptom that many high performers ignore. The need to stay awake, focused, or relaxed often leads individuals to rely on substances to get through the day. Over time, this can lead to physical dependence, where the individual feels they cannot function without the aid of the substance.

For example, Brian, a top consultant, relied heavily on caffeine to get through his 12-hour workdays. What began as a cup of coffee in the morning grew into multiple cups, energy drinks, and even caffeine supplements. Eventually, he found himself feeling jittery and unable to focus without a constant supply of caffeine. His dependence on the stimulant was so ingrained in his routine that he didn't recognize it as a problem. He convinced himself that it was simply part of his work routine and that he needed caffeine to perform at his best. However, the physical toll of his dependence on caffeine was beginning to impact his health and work performance.

Conclusion

The warning signs of dysfunction are often subtle and easy to ignore, especially for high performers who are driven by success and external validation. Emotional signs like burnout, numbness, and irritability are often dismissed as temporary setbacks, while physical signs like sleep issues, health decline, and substance dependence are easily explained away as part of the job. However, ignoring these warning signs only allows them to worsen over time. It is crucial for high achievers to recognize and address these signs early before they spiral into more serious consequences. Acknowledging the need for self-care, seeking help when necessary, and learning to manage stress in healthier ways are vital steps toward maintaining long-term success without sacrificing mental, emotional, or physical well-being.

Chapter 4

The Turning Point – Hitting a Different Kind of Bottom

Introduction

The term "rock bottom" is often associated with a dramatic collapse—a public spectacle of failure, a breakdown, or a crisis that becomes impossible to ignore. For many high achievers, however, the turning point comes not through a sudden and catastrophic event, but rather through a quiet unraveling, one that is slow, subtle, and often barely noticeable until it's too late. These individuals don't necessarily crash in the traditional sense; instead, they fade. They may seem to be functioning perfectly on the surface—continuing to excel in their careers, maintain relationships, and uphold their professional reputations—but internally, they are falling apart.

The quiet unraveling can be even more insidious than a dramatic crash because it is often mistaken for normal stress or pressure. It isn't always obvious, and it often happens over a long period of time. But as the emotional, psychological, and relational fabric of their lives begins to fray, the high achiever may start to question their purpose, their worth, and their place in the world. This chapter will explore the phenomenon of the "silent bottom," the subtle and often invisible decline that many successful individuals experience. It will also examine how this quiet unraveling impacts relationships, mental health, and self-worth, and tell stories of wake-up calls that serve as pivotal turning points on the journey to healing.

Not Everyone Crashes—Some Just Fade

It is common to think of rock bottom as a moment of explosive failure: a car accident, an intervention, a public meltdown, or a catastrophic loss of wealth or status. These events are often highly visible, and the individual's fall is immediate and obvious to everyone around them. However, not all high achievers experience this kind of dramatic descent. Many go through what could be called a "different kind of bottom," one that happens gradually and is far less noticeable. It is a process of fading rather than crashing, and it can be much harder to recognize.

Consider Emma, a renowned surgeon at a prestigious hospital. To the outside world, Emma had it all. She had a thriving career, a loving family, and the respect of her colleagues. However, over the years, her once-passionate dedication to her profession began to wane. She would arrive at the hospital exhausted, barely able to focus during surgeries, and retreat into isolation during her breaks. Her relationships with colleagues became strained, and she distanced herself from her family, no longer enjoying the things that once brought her joy. Emma wasn't experiencing a public collapse. She was still performing her duties, keeping up with the demands of her job, and maintaining a professional appearance. But internally, she was fading.

Emma's burnout wasn't an overnight event—it was a slow, creeping realization that her purpose and passion for her work had eroded over time. She had neglected her emotional well-being, focused solely on achieving more success in her career, and suppressed the feelings of exhaustion, disillusionment, and resentment that were slowly building within her. It wasn't until a routine checkup revealed a decline in her physical health—high blood pressure, sleep disturbances, and severe fatigue—that Emma was forced to confront the reality of her situation. Her "bottom" was not a single dramatic moment, but a gradual decline that had become too significant to ignore.

Emma's story is not unique. Many high achievers experience this slow fade, where they continue to "function" outwardly but gradually lose the passion, enthusiasm, and mental clarity that once defined their work and lives. For these individuals, the turning point often comes when they are forced to confront the consequences of their gradual unraveling, whether it is through health problems, personal crises, or moments of introspection that force them to reckon with the life they've been living.

The Quiet Unraveling: Relationships, Mental Health, Self-Worth

One of the most insidious aspects of the quiet unraveling is its impact on relationships, mental health, and self-worth. High achievers, who often derive their sense of identity and value from their success, may find themselves losing touch with the very things that matter most: meaningful relationships, a sense of purpose, and the ability to prioritize their mental and emotional well-being.

Relationships: The Silent Erosion of Connection

For high performers, relationships often take a backseat to career demands, especially in the early years of their professional journey. At first, the sacrifice seems manageable—long hours at work, missed social gatherings, and prioritizing professional success over personal time. But as time goes on, this imbalance can begin to erode relationships in ways that are subtle and easy to overlook.

Mark, a successful real estate developer, was known for his commitment to his career. He spent long hours traveling for work, meeting clients, and overseeing various projects. Initially, his wife, Sarah, supported his ambition, understanding that the sacrifices were temporary and that their future together would be brighter because of his hard work. But as the years passed, Sarah began to feel increasingly neglected. Mark was never home for dinner, and when he was, he was distracted, preoccupied with work emails and phone calls. They stopped having meaningful conversations, and the emotional intimacy that once bonded them began to fade.

For Mark, the deterioration of his marriage was gradual. He wasn't consciously neglecting Sarah, but his obsession with work made it impossible for him to prioritize his relationship. Sarah became resentful and frustrated, but she too kept her feelings hidden, not wanting to disrupt the family's stability. It wasn't until a crisis—when Sarah finally confronted him and told him she was thinking about leaving—that Mark realized how far things had deteriorated. The quiet unraveling of his relationship had been happening right before his eyes, but he had failed to see it until it reached a breaking point.

Mark's story illustrates how relationships can silently erode as high achievers continue to focus on success at the expense of their personal connections. The quiet unraveling of relationships often happens when one partner or friend feels unimportant, neglected, or emotionally unsupported. High achievers often neglect the emotional labor required to nurture their personal connections, and the result is a slow, quiet disintegration of the very relationships that are meant to provide love, support, and stability.

Mental Health: The Hidden Toll of Success

As high achievers continue to push themselves to meet external expectations, their mental health often begins to deteriorate. The pressure to constantly perform, to outdo oneself, and to keep up with an ever-demanding schedule can lead to stress, anxiety, and depression. However, many high performers refuse to acknowledge these mental health challenges, viewing them as signs of weakness or failure.

Rachel, a high-ranking marketing executive, was known for her drive and ambition. She thrived under pressure and had a reputation for always delivering results. But behind the scenes, Rachel struggled with feelings of anxiety and self-doubt. Despite her professional success, she felt like an imposter in her own life. She feared being exposed as inadequate, and as a result, she kept pushing herself harder. The anxiety that Rachel experienced on a daily basis was masked by her accomplishments—no one could see how deeply it affected her.

Rachel's mental health deteriorated over time. She became withdrawn, her sleep was disrupted, and she found it harder to focus during meetings. Her colleagues noticed a shift in her behavior, but Rachel refused to acknowledge what was happening. She was still performing at a high level, meeting deadlines, and impressing clients. It wasn't until she had a panic attack at work that she finally sought help. The realization that her mental health had been silently deteriorating for months came as a shock, but it was the wake-up call she needed to confront the toll her work was taking on her well-being.

Mental health issues like anxiety, depression, and burnout are common among high achievers, but they are often ignored or minimized. Many believe that their mental health struggles will disappear once they achieve their next goal, leading to a cycle of self-denial and avoidance. This silent decline in mental health can ultimately lead to a tipping point, where the individual is forced to reckon with the reality that their mental and emotional health cannot be neglected indefinitely.

Self-Worth: The Price of Perfection

One of the most dangerous aspects of the quiet unraveling is its impact on self-worth. High achievers often tie their sense of value to their accomplishments. Success is not just a measure of what they've done— it is who they are. As a result, when they experience failure, burnout, or emotional exhaustion, it can feel like a direct threat to their identity. Their self-worth becomes intertwined with their performance, and any deviation from perfection is seen as a failure.

David, a highly successful entrepreneur, had built his tech company from the ground up. For years, his sense of self was defined by the success of his business. He was driven by the belief that as long as his company was thriving, he was valuable. However, when his company hit a rough patch and he had to lay off employees, David felt like he had lost everything. His self-worth was shattered, and he struggled with feelings of shame and inadequacy. Despite the fact that his business was still functional and he had achieved great success, David couldn't shake the belief that he was no longer enough.

The erosion of self-worth is a powerful force in the quiet unraveling. When high achievers derive their sense of value from their accomplishments, any failure or setback can be devastating. The need to prove oneself and the fear of being "found out" can lead to chronic feelings of inadequacy and self-doubt. This internal struggle can become more pronounced over time, leading to a growing sense of emptiness and a fear that no amount of success will ever be enough.

Stories of Subtle but Powerful Wake-Up Calls

The turning point in many high achievers' journeys comes not through a catastrophic event, but through a quiet realization—a wake-up call that forces them to confront the damage they have done to themselves and their relationships. These wake-up calls are often subtle, but they have the power to catalyze change and help the individual recalibrate their priorities.

Liam, a successful consultant, had spent years climbing the corporate ladder, always striving for the next promotion or accolade. However, after a routine physical revealed troubling signs of stress-related health issues, Liam was forced to confront the toll his lifestyle had taken on his body. His doctor's stern warning about the potential long-term effects of his high-stress lifestyle was the wake-up call he needed. For the first time, Liam began to consider the possibility that his success was no longer worth the price he was paying. He realized that the "bottom" he had been inching toward was not a dramatic collapse, but a quiet decline that had gone unnoticed for far too long.

Similarly, Kate, an executive at a financial firm, experienced her wake-up call when her teenage daughter confronted her one evening. After years of missing family events, late nights at the office, and absent conversations at the dinner table, her daughter said, "I wish you would spend more time with us, Mom." That simple statement hit Kate like a ton of bricks. For the first time, she realized that her relentless pursuit of professional success had come at the expense of her family, and the realization of the emotional distance she had created was devastating. Kate's wake-up call wasn't a single event, but a quiet recognition of how her choices had affected those around her. It marked the beginning of her journey to redefine her priorities and seek a healthier work-life balance.

Conclusion

The turning point for high achievers often comes not through a dramatic crash, but through a quiet unraveling that is easy to ignore until the damage becomes too significant to overlook. The slow fade, marked by emotional exhaustion, deteriorating relationships, and a declining sense of self-worth, can be just as dangerous as a public collapse. The stories of subtle wake-up calls illustrate how high achievers can reach a turning point without experiencing the catastrophic crash that many associate with "rock bottom." Recognizing the warning signs of the quiet unraveling is crucial for maintaining long-term well-being. It is important for individuals to acknowledge that success, while important, should never come at the expense of mental health, relationships, and personal fulfillment. By confronting the quiet unraveling early, individuals can recalibrate their priorities and avoid hitting a different kind of bottom altogether.

Chapter 5
Admitting Without Falling Apart

Introduction

The road to self-awareness and healing is often paved with a powerful and, at times, terrifying moment of admission. That moment when you look at your reflection, face the uncomfortable reality, and finally say those words: "I have a problem." For many high achievers, this is the ultimate test—the acknowledgment that their carefully constructed world is unraveling, that the person they've presented to the world is not the whole truth, and that the façade they've maintained so diligently can no longer mask the pain, stress, and dysfunction that lie beneath.

Admitting a problem—whether it's an addiction, a mental health issue, or simply the overwhelming weight of unaddressed stress and burnout—can feel like a moment of vulnerability so profound that it threatens to strip away the very identity a person has built through years of hard work, discipline, and success. The fear is palpable: "If I admit this, will I lose everything?" The stakes feel impossibly high. Yet, paradoxically, it is often in this moment of admission that true healing can begin.

This chapter explores the challenges and fear that come with admitting a problem, how to seek help without feeling the crushing weight of shame, and how to create space for truth without losing one's identity. It delves into the critical steps of self-acceptance, finding the courage to reach out, and re-establishing one's sense of self when everything feels like it might come apart.

The Terrifying Confession: "I Have a Problem"

For high achievers, the confession "I have a problem" is not merely a verbal acknowledgment of a challenge—it is a monumental admission that directly challenges their sense of identity. Many high performers are conditioned to believe that they are the ones who solve problems, not the ones who have them. The idea of seeking help can feel like a personal defeat, an erosion of everything they've worked so hard to build. In many ways, admitting a problem feels like admitting failure. And in a world that celebrates achievement and success, failure is often the one thing high achievers are taught to avoid at all costs.

David, a senior partner at a prestigious law firm, had spent years building a reputation as one of the most successful and respected attorneys in his field. He had worked tirelessly to earn his position, sacrificing personal time, relationships, and even his health in the process. Yet, over time, David began to notice the signs of something deeper: anxiety that wouldn't let up, difficulty sleeping, and the constant compulsion to work, even when his body was screaming for rest. He didn't understand it at first. After all, his career was thriving. His financial success was unquestionable. Yet, something felt increasingly off.

It wasn't until he experienced a panic attack at the office that David could no longer deny the reality of his situation. Sitting in his car after the episode, he realized that the very thing he had spent his life building—his identity as a successful, high-achieving attorney—was built on a crumbling foundation. The realization that he had a problem was both humbling and terrifying. The walls of his self-image, which had been built on years of dedication, hard work, and achievement, were now being shattered by the admission that he was struggling and that he could no longer pretend everything was fine.

For many high performers like David, the process of admitting a problem is deeply frightening because it forces them to question the core of their identity. If success has been the cornerstone of your identity, admitting that something is wrong challenges everything you believe about yourself. It forces you to confront your vulnerabilities, weaknesses, and fears—the very things that have been hidden behind the polished surface of achievement.

How to Seek Help Without Shame

The fear of shame often prevents high achievers from seeking the help they need. Admitting a problem and seeking help can feel like a public declaration of failure. The cultural stigma surrounding vulnerability can create a sense of isolation, where individuals believe they must handle their struggles alone. For many high performers, the idea of seeking help seems counterintuitive to everything they've been taught. After all, they've spent their lives proving their strength, independence, and capability. To suddenly need help can feel like an admission of weakness.

However, seeking help is one of the most powerful and courageous acts a person can take. It is an acknowledgment that, despite all of one's success, it is okay to not have everything figured out. It is a reminder that being human means experiencing pain, struggle, and vulnerability. For high achievers, it's important to recognize that seeking help does not diminish their value or identity—it is, in fact, a strength.

Take the example of Susan, a high-level executive at a multinational corporation. Susan had long been admired for her leadership and sharp decision-making skills. Yet, over time, the pressure of her role began to take a toll. She felt exhausted, overwhelmed, and increasingly disconnected from her team. Despite the outward appearance of control, Susan began to recognize the signs of burnout: she was snapping at colleagues, losing her motivation, and struggling with feelings of inadequacy. It took months for her to admit that she was struggling, and even longer to acknowledge that she needed help.

When she finally reached out to a therapist, Susan was initially wracked with shame. "How could I let this happen?" she thought. "How can I be a leader and ask for help?" But the moment she allowed herself to speak the truth—to acknowledge that she was human, fallible, and in need of support—she began to experience a sense of relief. Seeking help was not a sign of failure but a step toward regaining control over her life. Through therapy, she learned how to set healthier boundaries, manage her stress, and reclaim a sense of balance. It was not an easy journey, but by seeking help without shame, Susan took the first step toward healing.

Seeking help doesn't have to be a public act or a grand declaration. It can begin in the privacy of a therapist's office, a support group, or even a trusted friend. The key is to understand that help is available, and asking for it is not a sign of weakness but an act of strength.

High performers may also struggle with the idea of vulnerability—especially when their success has been built on the image of invulnerability. However, vulnerability is often the first step toward real growth. It is in embracing vulnerability that individuals can begin to let go of the need for perfection, acknowledge their humanity, and find the support they need to heal. Vulnerability is not about being weak; it is about being honest.

Creating Space for Truth Without Losing Your Identity

For high achievers, the fear of losing their identity can be overwhelming. If you have spent years building a life and career based on external accomplishments, it can be terrifying to step back and examine the parts of your identity that have been neglected or hidden. The process of admitting a problem, seeking help, and exploring one's vulnerabilities can feel like an identity crisis, where the individual is forced to confront the possibility that their entire sense of self has been tied to something external: success, achievement, recognition, and productivity.

However, the truth is that identity is not solely built on external accomplishments. True self-worth comes from within, from the ability to acknowledge one's strengths and weaknesses, from the courage to be authentic, and from the commitment to grow. High achievers often confuse their identity with their achievements, but the process of admitting a problem and seeking help is an opportunity to redefine who they are at their core.

Tom, a successful entrepreneur, faced a similar crisis when he experienced a sudden breakdown. His business was thriving, his wealth was growing, and his reputation was solid. But deep inside, Tom felt like an imposter. He didn't feel fulfilled. He was constantly anxious and restless. His emotional and mental health had been deteriorating, and yet, he had convinced himself that as long as his business succeeded, everything would be fine.

After seeking help and going through therapy, Tom realized that he had built his entire identity around his business success. He had neglected his own needs, values, and desires in the process. Through therapy, he learned that he could create space for truth without losing his identity. He did not have to be defined solely by his entrepreneurial achievements. Instead, he began to rediscover parts of himself that had been neglected—his passions, his sense of purpose, and his relationships.

The process of creating space for truth—allowing oneself to be vulnerable and honest—does not mean losing your identity. It means shedding the layers of external validation and reconnecting with your authentic self. High achievers often live in a constant state of doing, measuring, and achieving, but true healing comes from embracing being—not just doing. It is in these quiet moments of introspection, of admitting the things that hurt and acknowledging the areas where growth is needed, that individuals can rediscover their core identity. They can begin to see themselves not just as the sum of their achievements but as complex, multi-dimensional individuals with the capacity for change, growth, and resilience.

Conclusion

The moment of admitting a problem is often the most challenging and terrifying moment in a high achiever's journey. For many, it feels like the collapse of their identity, the unraveling of everything they've worked so hard to build. However, this moment is not a sign of failure—it is the beginning of the path to healing. Seeking help without shame, creating space for truth, and redefining one's identity are all essential components of this process.

Admitting that you have a problem is not an easy step, especially for those who have spent their lives building a reputation of strength and success. Yet, in facing the truth, high achievers can reclaim their sense of self, embrace vulnerability, and embark on a journey of healing that leads to a more balanced, authentic, and fulfilling life.

Chapter 6

Detoxing While Holding a Briefcase

Introduction

For high performers—whether they're business executives, entrepreneurs, or top-tier professionals—the path to recovery is uniquely complicated. The very nature of their success, the demands of their work, and the high expectations placed on them can make it difficult to take the necessary steps toward healing. The idea of detoxing or seeking treatment often feels like a paradox. How can someone dedicated to their career or business take time to recover without losing everything they've worked so hard to build? The fear of falling behind, losing status, or being judged by colleagues and clients can be overwhelming.

Yet, the need for treatment—whether for addiction, burnout, or mental health challenges—doesn't disappear because someone has a briefcase to carry. High achievers often face the difficult challenge of balancing their recovery journey with their professional responsibilities. The prospect of detoxing while managing a career or running a business can feel like walking a tightrope. The key to navigating this delicate balance lies in understanding the available treatment options, knowing when to seek help, and finding strategies that allow for healing without sacrificing one's career or sense of identity.

In this chapter, we will explore how professionals can navigate treatment while keeping their career or business afloat, compare outpatient and inpatient options for treatment, and discuss the benefits and limitations of executive recovery programs designed specifically for high achievers.

Navigating Treatment While Keeping Your Career or Business Afloat

For high performers, the idea of taking time off to attend a treatment program often feels like an impossible decision. The demands of the job are constant, the stakes are high, and there is a real fear of falling behind. They may worry that if they take time away, their colleagues will question their competence, their clients will lose confidence, or their business will suffer irreparably. But the reality is that the decision to seek treatment is not just about healing—it's about preserving the long-term sustainability of their career, business, and overall well-being.

Take the case of Richard, a CEO of a growing tech company. He had built the company from the ground up, and his leadership was central to its success. However, over time, the pressures of managing a rapidly expanding business, coupled with his increasing reliance on alcohol to cope with stress, began to take a toll on his physical and mental health. He knew he needed help, but the thought of stepping away from the company seemed impossible. If he left, who would make the crucial decisions? How would the company continue to function without him at the helm? Richard's story is not unique—many high achievers face the dilemma of wanting to seek help but feeling tied to their work and career.

To navigate this, professionals must first confront the reality that their health and well-being are the foundation of their ability to perform at a high level. Without addressing the underlying issues, burnout or addiction will continue to chip away at their effectiveness, relationships, and long-term success. The choice to seek treatment is not one that should be made lightly, but it is also not one that should be avoided out of fear.

One strategy for balancing recovery with career responsibilities is to carefully plan the timing and structure of treatment. For instance, Richard decided to seek outpatient treatment for alcohol dependence, which allowed him to attend therapy and support meetings during the evening while still managing his work responsibilities during the day. This flexibility helped him begin his recovery without putting his company at risk. Outpatient programs allow individuals to receive treatment while maintaining their work schedule, providing the necessary support while still keeping their professional life intact.

Another approach is to delegate or temporarily hand over key responsibilities to trusted team members. This allows high performers to step back without leaving a vacuum in their business or career. Richard took the step of promoting a trusted senior executive to temporarily assume some of his leadership responsibilities while he focused on his recovery. By building a strong leadership team and empowering others, professionals can ensure that their absence doesn't result in a collapse of operations.

Outpatient vs. Inpatient Options for Professionals

When considering treatment, one of the first decisions professionals must make is whether outpatient or inpatient care is the best option for them. Both have their advantages and challenges, and the choice largely depends on the severity of the issue at hand, the individual's capacity to manage their professional responsibilities, and their personal preferences.

Outpatient Treatment

Outpatient treatment is often a preferred option for high achievers who cannot afford to take extended time away from their professional lives. In outpatient programs, individuals receive treatment during scheduled sessions (typically weekly or multiple times a week) but can continue living at home, attending work, and maintaining some of their professional duties. This option is ideal for those whose conditions are less severe, or for individuals who feel they can maintain a certain level of functionality while receiving care.

For someone like Rachel, a highly successful marketing executive, outpatient treatment was the perfect choice. Rachel had been battling anxiety and burnout for years, but she still needed to manage her business relationships and maintain her work responsibilities. Outpatient treatment allowed her to attend therapy sessions during lunch breaks or in the evenings, receiving the support she needed without completely stepping away from her role. She also participated in group therapy and individual counseling sessions, which helped her gain new coping strategies and perspectives on managing stress.

One of the key benefits of outpatient treatment is its flexibility. It allows individuals to continue with their careers and responsibilities while addressing the root causes of their struggles. However, this flexibility also means that individuals need to be highly disciplined in balancing their professional duties with their personal recovery. The temptation to overwork or neglect recovery obligations can be a significant challenge.

Another challenge with outpatient treatment is that individuals are still exposed to the same pressures and stressors that contributed to their issues in the first place. For someone like Rachel, the constant pressure of delivering results and managing a team could exacerbate her anxiety. The success of outpatient treatment depends largely on the individual's ability to set boundaries, prioritize self-care, and maintain a strong commitment to their healing process.

Inpatient Treatment

Inpatient treatment, or residential treatment, involves individuals checking into a treatment facility for an extended period (typically 30 to 90 days) to receive 24/7 care. This option is often recommended for individuals dealing with more severe conditions—such as addiction, extreme burnout, or mental health crises—that require intensive, immersive care. Inpatient treatment provides a structured environment where individuals can focus entirely on their recovery, without the distractions and pressures of their career or business responsibilities.

For someone like Michael, a corporate executive suffering from severe addiction, inpatient treatment was the best choice. Michael had reached a point where his addiction was interfering with his ability to function at work, and he needed to remove himself from the pressures of daily life to begin the healing process. Inpatient treatment allowed Michael to receive daily therapy, medical support, and the time he needed to detoxify both physically and emotionally. The immersive nature of inpatient care provided the space for Michael to focus solely on his recovery, without the distractions of emails, meetings, or deadlines.

While inpatient treatment offers a more intensive and focused environment, it also presents significant challenges for professionals. The most obvious challenge is the time commitment. For high achievers, taking 30 to 90 days away from their business or career can feel like an insurmountable obstacle. The fear of losing ground, disappointing clients, or being seen as weak can deter many professionals from choosing this route. However, inpatient treatment can be incredibly effective in breaking the cycle of addiction or burnout and providing a comprehensive recovery program that addresses both the physical and emotional aspects of the issue.

Another challenge of inpatient treatment is the potential stigma. For some professionals, the idea of being away from their career or business for an extended period can feel like admitting failure. It's important for individuals to remember that recovery is an investment in their long-term health and well-being, and seeking inpatient care is a proactive step toward reclaiming their life and career.

Executive Recovery Programs: Benefits and Limitations

Executive recovery programs are designed specifically for high-level professionals, offering tailored treatment plans that take into account the unique pressures and demands of their careers. These programs often provide a more flexible approach to recovery, allowing individuals to receive treatment while still managing their business responsibilities. Executive recovery programs may include outpatient therapy, group sessions, and coaching, as well as additional support tailored to the needs of high performers.

Benefits of Executive Recovery Programs

One of the primary benefits of executive recovery programs is the understanding that professionals need to maintain their work commitments while also addressing their health challenges. These programs often provide specialized care that is mindful of the pressures that come with high-level positions. Executive recovery programs are designed to help individuals manage their recovery in a way that doesn't interfere with their work responsibilities, allowing them to continue leading and performing at a high level while undergoing treatment.

For example, some executive recovery programs offer a combination of individual therapy, group sessions, and coaching, along with regular check-ins to monitor progress. The goal is to help individuals navigate their personal challenges while providing support in managing the unique stressors of their professional roles. These programs also often offer a discrete and private environment, where high achievers can receive care without the fear of their struggles becoming public knowledge.

Executive recovery programs may also include specific tools and resources aimed at improving productivity and stress management. By focusing on the professional needs of the individual, these programs can help high achievers rebuild their confidence and skills in managing their workload, relationships, and personal well-being. This holistic approach ensures that individuals not only recover but thrive in their professional and personal lives.

Limitations of Executive Recovery Programs

Despite the advantages, executive recovery programs also come with their limitations. The most significant challenge is that these programs often focus primarily on managing the individual's symptoms, rather than addressing the root causes of their struggles. For some professionals, the recovery process may require more intensive, long-term care that cannot be adequately addressed through executive-focused programs alone.

Additionally, the focus on professional success in executive recovery programs can sometimes lead to a reinforcement of the very workaholic mindset that contributed to the individual's struggles in the first place. While these programs offer valuable support, there is a risk that they may inadvertently prioritize professional success over emotional and psychological healing.

Finally, executive recovery programs can be expensive, and the privacy and exclusivity of these programs may not always be accessible to everyone. High-performing professionals who are struggling with financial strain may find it difficult to justify the cost of these specialized programs.

Conclusion

For high achievers, navigating treatment while managing a career or business is a delicate balance. Whether opting for outpatient or inpatient treatment, or choosing a specialized executive recovery program, the journey to healing requires careful planning, dedication, and self-compassion. Detoxing while holding a briefcase is not about choosing between career success and personal health; it is about finding a way to integrate both. By recognizing the importance of recovery and making the decision to prioritize personal well-being, professionals can continue to thrive in their careers without sacrificing their health or happiness. The road to recovery may be challenging, but it is also an opportunity to rediscover balance, reestablish boundaries, and create a sustainable future where both career and personal well-being can coexist.

Chapter 7

Brainpower in Recovery

Introduction

For high achievers, intelligence is both a gift and a curse. On one hand, the ability to think critically, solve complex problems, and stay ahead of the curve is a source of strength. On the other hand, the same qualities that allow these individuals to succeed can often hinder their ability to recover from the very challenges they face. For many high performers, their intelligence, drive, and relentless pursuit of success can become double-edged swords. These attributes may help them navigate their professional worlds with remarkable efficiency, but when it comes to recovery—whether from addiction, burnout, or mental health struggles—their mental acuity can become an obstacle.

This chapter explores how a high IQ and intense drive can both help and hurt professionals in the recovery process. It delves into the ways overthinking, over-researching, and the resistance to vulnerability can complicate healing, and offers strategies for using intelligence in a constructive way to build smart, sustainable recovery plans. Recovery is not just about addressing the surface symptoms; it's about reshaping how high performers approach their own healing. leveraging their brainpower to create new pathways toward self-care, emotional well-being, and sustainable success.

How Your High IQ and Drive Can Help—and Hurt You

For many high achievers, their intellectual capabilities and drive are the engines that fuel their success. They've spent years honing their skills, solving problems, and navigating complex environments. These strengths allow them to thrive in demanding professional roles, to excel in challenging environments, and to outperform their peers. However, the very traits that make them successful in their careers can sometimes hinder their recovery journey.

The Strengths of Intelligence and Drive

Intelligence is a tool that can be incredibly helpful in recovery. High achievers who possess the ability to analyze, evaluate, and strategize are well-positioned to take an organized and thoughtful approach to their healing process. This means they can identify the root causes of their struggles, break down the recovery process into manageable steps, and find solutions that are tailored to their specific needs.

Take, for example, Jack, a renowned software engineer. Jack's ability to think analytically helped him identify early on that his reliance on caffeine and late-night work habits were contributing to his anxiety and burnout. With his high IQ and keen problem-solving skills, Jack was able to research methods for managing stress, prioritizing sleep, and improving his time management. His ability to critically assess his behavior allowed him to understand the factors that were exacerbating his issues and take proactive steps to address them.

Moreover, high achievers' drive and ambition are often their greatest assets in recovery. These individuals are used to striving for excellence and pushing through obstacles to reach their goals. This relentless determination can be a key asset in recovery. Once they commit to getting better, they often pour the same energy into their recovery as they would into a business project, making progress more quickly than others who may not have the same level of drive. This drive allows them to take charge of their recovery, whether that means adhering to a strict treatment plan, attending therapy sessions consistently, or investing time and resources into self-care practices.

The Downsides of Overthinking and Overanalyzing

Despite these strengths, the very qualities that make high achievers successful can also create significant barriers in the recovery process. One of the most notable downsides is overthinking.

Overthinking, or the tendency to excessively analyze and dwell on thoughts, decisions, and possibilities, can derail the recovery process. High achievers, accustomed to finding answers to complex problems, may believe that they can think their way out of emotional challenges. They may try to logically dissect every feeling, every trigger, and every symptom, overanalyzing situations rather than addressing them in a more holistic or emotional way.

Consider Sarah, an executive who was battling burnout. She was constantly overthinking her recovery process. Instead of simply attending therapy or participating in a mindfulness practice, she spent hours researching the latest psychological models, stress-reduction techniques, and recovery strategies. While this research is helpful to some extent, Sarah's tendency to overanalyze every option left her paralyzed. She would research and try to create a perfect plan for recovery, yet she often found herself stuck in indecision, unable to commit to any one path. The pursuit of the "right" answer became a source of additional stress, and the action that was necessary for her healing became delayed.

Overthinking can also lead to "analysis paralysis," where the individual becomes so focused on understanding the problem that they fail to take any meaningful steps toward resolution. This mental spiral can prevent high achievers from moving forward in their recovery, leaving them in a perpetual state of confusion and self-doubt.

Over-Researching and Resistance to Vulnerability

Another downside of high intelligence is the tendency to over-research recovery options, believing that more information will bring clarity and solutions. High achievers are often used to solving problems by gathering as much data as possible. This might work in professional scenarios, where detailed information is essential, but when it comes to emotional health and recovery, this approach can backfire.

Take, for example, David, a successful entrepreneur who had struggled with addiction for years. When he finally admitted he needed help, his first instinct was to start researching every addiction treatment program, reading books on addiction, and listening to podcasts about recovery. While information is valuable, David's incessant need to gather more data about addiction and recovery only fueled his anxiety. He became fixated on finding the "perfect" treatment method and became increasingly overwhelmed by the many options available. His intellectual drive led him to resist taking any concrete action, as he believed he needed more information before making a decision.

This over-researching tendency can also fuel resistance to vulnerability. High achievers, who are often admired for their mental fortitude and logical thinking, may resist the emotional side of recovery. They may view vulnerability as a weakness or fear that they will be seen as less competent or capable. Admitting that they need help, or that they don't have all the answers, can feel like a direct threat to their identity as capable, high-functioning individuals. This resistance to vulnerability can prevent them from fully engaging in the recovery process.

For instance, Olivia, a top-tier consultant, struggled with feelings of shame and inadequacy when she was advised to attend group therapy. Her intelligence told her that she could handle her issues independently—why should she need the support of others? She felt uncomfortable sharing her struggles with a group, believing that doing so would expose her as weak or less competent. This resistance to vulnerability slowed her progress in therapy, as she refused to open up fully, even though she understood the intellectual value of group therapy.

Using Intelligence to Build Smart Recovery Strategies

Although the tendencies of overthinking, over-researching, and resisting vulnerability can be hindrances, high achievers can leverage their intelligence to create effective recovery strategies. The key is learning to apply their intellectual skills in a way that complements, rather than complicates, their healing process. Here are a few strategies for using intelligence constructively in recovery:

1. Set Clear, Realistic Goals

High achievers are used to setting ambitious goals, but in the context of recovery, it's crucial to set clear and achievable goals that focus on progress, not perfection. Recovery is not a linear process, and trying to measure success by strict benchmarks can lead to frustration and burnout. Instead, intelligent recovery plans focus on small, manageable steps that promote growth over time.

For example, instead of aiming to "completely eliminate stress" or "perfectly balance work and personal life," professionals can set specific, realistic goals such as "attend one therapy session per week" or "practice mindfulness for 10 minutes daily." By breaking down the recovery process into smaller, digestible goals, individuals can avoid the pressure of achieving perfection and focus on steady progress.

2. Integrate Cognitive Behavioral Techniques

High achievers can benefit from applying their problem-solving skills to cognitive-behavioral strategies. Cognitive-behavioral therapy (CBT) helps individuals identify negative thought patterns and replace them with healthier, more constructive thinking. Intelligent individuals can use their analytical mindset to engage in this process by examining their thoughts and behaviors, identifying triggers, and systematically changing their responses.

For instance, when experiencing anxiety or stress, a high achiever can use CBT techniques to identify irrational or unhelpful thoughts and replace them with more realistic and calming thoughts. By using intelligence to work through these cognitive processes, individuals can break free from the cycles of overthinking that often hold them back.

3. Leverage Strengths in Time Management and Prioritization

High achievers are typically skilled at time management and prioritization, and these skills can be directly applied to recovery. Creating a structured plan that allocates time for self-care, therapy, rest, and other recovery activities can help individuals avoid burnout and stay on track. By viewing recovery as a project that requires careful planning and time management, high performers can bring the same level of organization to their healing as they do to their professional endeavors.

For example, an executive recovering from burnout can structure their day to include work tasks, recovery activities, and rest periods. They can use their time management skills to avoid over-scheduling and ensure that they have adequate time to focus on both their work and personal well-being.

4. Practice Mindfulness and Acceptance

One of the most important aspects of recovery is learning to accept vulnerability and the unpredictable nature of healing. Mindfulness techniques—such as meditation, deep breathing, or yoga—can help high achievers ground themselves in the present moment and embrace their emotional experiences without judgment. Rather than overanalyzing their thoughts or emotions, high performers can use mindfulness to simply observe and accept their feelings without trying to control or fix them.

By applying their intelligence to understanding mindfulness techniques, high achievers can begin to reframe their thinking about vulnerability and learn that emotional openness is not a sign of weakness, but a necessary step toward true healing.

Conclusion

Brainpower can be a powerful ally in recovery, but for high achievers, it can also become a double-edged sword. Intelligence, drive, and critical thinking skills can help individuals identify solutions and take charge of their healing process, but they can also lead to overthinking, over-researching, and resistance to vulnerability. The key to successful recovery lies in learning how to channel these attributes constructively. By setting clear goals, using cognitive-behavioral techniques, leveraging time management skills, and practicing mindfulness, high achievers can use their intellectual strengths to build smart, sustainable recovery strategies. Recovery doesn't have to be a battle between intellect and emotion—it's about learning to integrate both in a way that promotes healing, growth, and long-term well-being.

Chapter 8

Your Ego Is Not Your Enemy—Until It Is

Introduction

Ego—the part of the self that is concerned with identity, pride, and self-worth—can be a double-edged sword. At its best, it drives individuals to achieve greatness, to rise above challenges, and to push beyond limits. It is the inner voice that says, "I can do this" and "I am capable," and it plays a crucial role in building confidence and resilience. For high achievers, ego often becomes the fuel that propels them toward their goals. It shapes the very foundation of their drive, ambition, and success.

But ego can also be a formidable barrier. When unchecked, it can lead to pride, defensiveness, and an inflated sense of control that prevents growth and healing. Ego, when allowed to dominate, becomes an enemy—one that resists vulnerability, stifles humility, and keeps individuals trapped in a cycle of perfectionism, fear of failure, and self-doubt. The challenge, then, is not to eradicate the ego but to understand how it operates, learn how to manage it, and embrace the humility and vulnerability necessary for true growth.

In this chapter, we will explore how ego, when left unchecked, can sabotage recovery, relationships, and success. We will delve into the ways in which pride, control, and fear of failure fuel ego-driven behaviors and discuss how high achievers can break through these barriers. Furthermore, we will explore how to learn humility without losing confidence and how to redefine strength in vulnerability—shifting the perception of strength from an image of invulnerability to one of emotional openness and self-awareness.

Breaking Through Pride, Control, and Fear of Failure

One of the primary ways that ego becomes an obstacle is through pride. Pride, in this context, is the inflated sense of self-importance that causes individuals to overestimate their abilities or feel above certain tasks. High achievers, who have spent years developing their expertise and rising through the ranks, are particularly vulnerable to pride. They may believe that asking for help, acknowledging vulnerability, or admitting a need for change is a sign of weakness. In many cases, pride is deeply intertwined with their sense of identity—if they let go of their pride, they risk losing their status, reputation, or self-image.

Take the case of Peter, a successful investment banker who had climbed the corporate ladder quickly. He was known for his sharp mind, impeccable decision-making, and ability to handle high-pressure situations. Peter's pride in his success was palpable; it was woven into every aspect of his personality. When he faced a series of personal setbacks, including the collapse of a business venture, his initial instinct was to distance himself from the situation. He refused to admit that he was struggling, convinced that he should have all the answers. Asking for help, he believed, would tarnish his reputation and make him appear incompetent.

Peter's story illustrates how pride can prevent growth and healing. By refusing to confront his vulnerabilities and embrace the possibility of failure, Peter trapped himself in a cycle of isolation and denial. His ego fueled his resistance to change and kept him from addressing the underlying issues that were affecting both his personal life and his professional success.

Pride often leads to another obstacle—control. For high achievers, control is an essential part of their identity. They are used to managing their circumstances, making decisions, and executing plans with precision. However, when ego drives the need for control, it can manifest in unhealthy ways. The need for perfectionism, the refusal to delegate, and the overwhelming desire to keep everything under control can create a barrier to recovery.

Consider Anna, an accomplished entrepreneur who had built a successful startup. As her business grew, so did her sense of control. She believed that in order for the company to succeed, she needed to have her hands in every part of the operation—oversight on every decision, micromanaging her team, and making every major call. This intense need for control came at the cost of her mental health and relationships. She struggled with stress, burnout, and exhaustion but continued to push forward, convinced that if she didn't control every detail, the business would fail. Anna's ego led her to believe that her identity was tied to the company's success, and her pride in managing everything herself became a source of personal pride.

In both Peter and Anna's cases, their ego-driven need for control prevented them from acknowledging the realities of their situation. Their belief that they had to "do it all" created additional pressure, leading them further away from healing and self-acceptance. Instead of embracing vulnerability or seeking support, they clung to the illusion that they had to maintain control at all costs.

Finally, ego often feeds into the fear of failure. For many high achievers, failure is the one thing they cannot bear to face. Failure threatens their identity and challenges their deeply held belief that success is the measure of their worth. This fear of failure can lead to procrastination, perfectionism, and avoidance—further fueling the ego's need to protect itself from perceived threats.

Consider David, an attorney who had always been lauded for his quick thinking and sharp legal mind. He had a string of victories in court and a reputation for being one of the top lawyers in his firm. However, when faced with a particularly challenging case, David found himself paralyzed by the fear of failure. His ego told him that he had to win at all costs, or he would lose his standing in the firm and his sense of self-worth. As a result, David spent countless hours over-preparing, obsessing over every detail, and resisting the idea that failure might be a possibility. This fear of failure not only strained his mental health but also kept him from thinking creatively and making the best decisions.

David's fear of failure, driven by his ego, ultimately worked against him. Instead of embracing the possibility of failure as a learning experience, he allowed his ego to dictate his actions, leading to increased stress, anxiety, and poor performance.

Learning Humility Without Losing Confidence

Humility is one of the most important qualities to cultivate in recovery. It is the ability to recognize one's limitations, acknowledge mistakes, and be open to learning and growth. Humility is the antidote to pride and ego-driven behaviors—it allows individuals to embrace vulnerability, accept help, and take the necessary steps toward healing.

However, learning humility does not mean abandoning confidence. High achievers often tie their self-worth to their abilities and achievements, and it can be difficult to reconcile the need for humility with the need for self-assurance. The key is to understand that humility is not about diminishing one's abilities or downplaying achievements. It is about recognizing that no one is invincible, and that true strength lies in the ability to be open, self-aware, and willing to grow.

For example, George, a CEO who had built a successful international brand, struggled with the idea of humility. Throughout his career, he had been celebrated for his leadership and vision. However, as the company faced significant challenges, George's pride and fear of failure prevented him from seeking support or listening to his team. It wasn't until he had a candid conversation with a trusted advisor that he began to realize how his ego had clouded his judgment. The advisor gently reminded him that seeking help, listening to others, and acknowledging his vulnerabilities were signs of true leadership. George was able to take this advice to heart and began to embrace humility without losing his confidence. By acknowledging his limitations and accepting feedback, George became a more effective leader and a more self-aware individual.

Learning humility requires the ability to separate one's identity from external achievements. High achievers who learn to embrace humility are not diminishing their worth—they are simply acknowledging that their value is not solely defined by their professional success. Humility allows them to embrace imperfection and vulnerability without fearing that they are losing their identity. It is a mindset shift that fosters growth and resilience, helping individuals navigate recovery with greater ease and openness.

Redefining Strength in Vulnerability

One of the most profound shifts that high achievers must make in recovery is redefining strength. For many professionals, strength has always been synonymous with control, perfection, and invulnerability. Strength means never admitting weakness, never asking for help, and never letting others see your flaws. However, this definition of strength is rooted in ego and is ultimately unsustainable. True strength comes from the ability to be vulnerable—to acknowledge your struggles, face your fears, and ask for help when needed.

Vulnerability is often viewed as a weakness, especially in high-performance cultures that celebrate perfection and achievement. But in reality, vulnerability is the cornerstone of emotional resilience. It is the willingness to open oneself up to the possibility of failure, to embrace imperfection, and to acknowledge that healing requires help from others. For high achievers, learning to embrace vulnerability is a powerful way to redefine strength—not as a façade of invulnerability, but as the courage to face one's challenges head-on.

Take the example of Lily, a highly respected surgeon who had always prided herself on her expertise and ability to perform under pressure. When Lily faced a personal crisis, she initially resisted the idea of seeking therapy, believing that it would make her appear weak. However, after much internal struggle, she realized that her emotional health was just as important as her professional performance. She sought therapy and began to open up about her fears, her stress, and the pressure she felt to maintain an image of perfection. Through therapy, Lily came to understand that vulnerability was not a sign of weakness, but an opportunity to build deeper emotional strength. By embracing vulnerability, she was able to rebuild her confidence, improve her relationships, and find greater balance in her life.

The key to redefining strength lies in recognizing that true strength comes from within. It is not about controlling everything or always appearing flawless—it is about the courage to be open, to acknowledge one's struggles, and to seek help when necessary. Vulnerability is not a weakness; it is the path to growth, healing, and self-awareness.

Conclusion

Ego can be both a powerful asset and a formidable obstacle in the recovery process. When managed well, it drives success, ambition, and personal growth. But when left unchecked, it can lead to pride, control, and fear of failure—barriers that prevent true healing and self-acceptance. High achievers must learn to break through these ego-driven obstacles by embracing humility, learning to balance confidence with vulnerability, and redefining strength as the courage to confront one's weaknesses. True strength comes not from invulnerability, but from the willingness to face challenges with openness, self-awareness, and a commitment to growth. By managing their ego in recovery, high achievers can navigate their healing journey with greater resilience, emotional balance, and long-term success.

Chapter 9

Rewiring the Reward System

Introduction

The human brain is wired for reward. We all seek pleasure and avoid pain, and this basic drive shapes many of our decisions, behaviors, and habits. The brain's reward system—the complex network of structures and chemicals that make us feel good when we achieve something or experience pleasure—plays a crucial role in both our successes and our struggles. For high achievers, this reward system can be a double-edged sword. While it motivates us to perform at our best and accomplish great things, it can also lead us into patterns of unhealthy behavior when we begin to rely on substances or behaviors that provide a quick, intense sense of reward.

For those in recovery—whether from addiction, burnout, or mental health struggles—rewiring the reward system becomes an essential part of the healing process. This chapter explores how individuals can replace unhealthy substances or behaviors with healthy "highs," learn to hack their dopamine system through positive activities like exercise, creativity, and connection, and build lasting resilience through consistency rather than intensity.

Replacing Substances or Behaviors with Healthy Highs

One of the most significant challenges in recovery is learning how to replace the unhealthy rewards that substances or behaviors once provided with healthier, more sustainable sources of pleasure and fulfillment. Whether it's the immediate "high" from alcohol, drugs, gambling, or even workaholism, these quick fixes activate the brain's reward system in ways that feel gratifying in the moment but ultimately leave individuals feeling empty, exhausted, or worse off.

In recovery, the goal is to replace these addictive behaviors with activities that also trigger the brain's reward system, but in ways that support long-term well-being rather than short-term gratification. The key is to find new ways of achieving the same sense of reward—whether that's the rush of excitement, the sense of accomplishment, or the emotional comfort that unhealthy behaviors once provided.

Take the example of Robert, a high-level executive who had struggled with alcohol addiction for years. Robert had always relied on alcohol to unwind after long, stressful workdays. The quick, euphoric rush of drinking provided temporary relief from the pressures of his job, but it also led to a cycle of physical and emotional dependency. When Robert entered recovery, he had to learn how to replace alcohol with healthier "highs"—activities that would give him a similar sense of satisfaction without the negative consequences.

Initially, Robert struggled with this shift. He found that exercise—something he had always neglected—provided a healthy release. Running, hiking, and yoga became his new sources of dopamine, and he began to appreciate the sense of accomplishment that came from pushing himself physically. Not only did exercise provide a natural high, but it also helped reduce the anxiety and stress that had once led him to drink. Over time, Robert began to incorporate other rewarding activities into his routine, including journaling, spending time with family, and pursuing creative hobbies that allowed him to express himself in new ways.

The key to replacing unhealthy rewards is not about completely eliminating pleasure or enjoyment; it's about finding healthier sources of reward that align with the goals of recovery. Activities like exercise, hobbies, and social connection can trigger the same pleasure pathways in the brain as substances or addictive behaviors, but they offer lasting benefits that promote emotional, physical, and mental well-being.

Hacking Dopamine: Exercise, Creativity, and Connection

The brain's primary "feel-good" chemical, dopamine, plays a central role in our reward system. Dopamine is released when we achieve something, experience pleasure, or engage in activities that provide a sense of satisfaction or excitement. It is the brain's way of reinforcing behaviors that help us survive, grow, and thrive. However, the challenge in recovery is learning how to hack this system in healthy ways, especially when the brain has been conditioned to seek instant gratification from substances or harmful behaviors.

Exercise: The Dopamine Boost You Can't Ignore

Exercise is one of the most effective ways to hack the brain's dopamine system. Physical activity increases the release of dopamine, along with other "feel-good" chemicals like serotonin and endorphins. For individuals in recovery, exercise provides a natural, sustainable source of reward that not only boosts mood but also improves physical health and reduces stress.

Consider Emily, an attorney who had spent years struggling with workaholism and stress. Emily had always prided herself on her career, but the pressure of her job led to burnout and eventually, feelings of depression and anxiety. In her recovery journey, Emily discovered the power of exercise as a tool for emotional and mental healing. She began incorporating daily runs into her routine, and over time, she noticed that exercise provided her with a sense of relief from the emotional weight she had carried. The physical exertion triggered dopamine release, boosting her mood and making her feel more in control of her emotions.

Exercise, especially cardiovascular activities like running, swimming, or cycling, offers a powerful way to trigger dopamine release in a healthy, sustainable way. It provides immediate positive feedback, boosting mood and energy levels, while also having long-term benefits for overall health, resilience, and well-being. For many high achievers in recovery, exercise becomes an essential part of their routine—helping them replace unhealthy habits with positive, rewarding behaviors.

Creativity: Engaging the Brain in New Ways

Creativity is another powerful tool for hacking dopamine. Engaging in creative activities—whether that's painting, writing, playing music, or designing—activates the brain's reward system and provides a sense of accomplishment. Creative pursuits allow individuals to express themselves, explore new ideas, and experience the joy of making something unique, all while boosting dopamine levels.

For example, Alex, a successful but stressed-out graphic designer, found that her work was no longer providing the fulfillment it once had. She had become disconnected from her passion for design and felt increasingly burnt out by the constant pressure to deliver. As part of her recovery, Alex decided to explore painting as a way to reconnect with her creativity. She began dedicating time each week to paint freely, without the pressure of meeting client demands or deadlines. The act of creating art—not for validation or profit, but for personal enjoyment—triggered a sense of satisfaction and pride that she hadn't felt in years. Each brushstroke brought a release of dopamine, boosting her mood and sense of well-being.

Creativity is not just about producing something beautiful or useful—it's about engaging the brain in new and fulfilling ways. Whether it's crafting, writing, dancing, or any other form of self-expression, creative activities help individuals tap into the brain's reward system without relying on substances or unhealthy behaviors. For high achievers in recovery, creativity offers a way to reconnect with their passions, reduce stress, and experience the joy of creation.

Connection: Building Social Bonds and Sharing Experiences

Social connection is one of the most powerful ways to hack the dopamine system, and for those in recovery, it is an essential part of healing. Human beings are wired for connection—dopamine is released when we interact with others, form bonds, and share experiences. In the context of recovery, building a strong social support network is critical to long-term success. Social connections provide a sense of belonging, validation, and emotional support, all of which are essential for healing.

For Mark, a successful businessman who had struggled with isolation and addiction, building deeper connections with others became a key part of his recovery. He began to attend support groups and reconnect with friends and family members he had neglected over the years. Sharing his experiences with others, hearing their stories, and offering support in return became a source of reward that triggered the release of dopamine. Mark realized that his social connections were not only vital for emotional healing but also provided a sustainable source of pleasure and satisfaction that he had been missing.

Building meaningful connections in recovery can be transformative. Whether through support groups, family gatherings, or friendships, social interactions provide a sense of purpose, connection, and joy that cannot be replicated by substances or unhealthy behaviors. For high achievers, learning to prioritize authentic connections over work or external success is a crucial part of building resilience and maintaining long-term recovery.

Building Resilience Through Consistency, Not Intensity

In the pursuit of recovery, high achievers are often accustomed to intensity. They are used to working long hours, pushing themselves to the limit, and expecting rapid results. This drive for intensity can be useful in professional settings, but it is not always the most effective approach when it comes to recovery. Building resilience in recovery is not about pushing oneself harder or expecting quick fixes—it's about consistency.

Consistency is the foundation of sustainable recovery. It's the daily, incremental steps that build momentum over time. Rather than focusing on dramatic, intense efforts to change everything at once, high achievers should focus on small, manageable changes that can be maintained over the long term. Consistency allows individuals to build positive habits that support their recovery, gradually rewiring the brain's reward system and reinforcing healthy behaviors.

For example, Mia, a successful entrepreneur, had always approached life with intensity. When she decided to tackle her burnout and stress, she initially threw herself into an intense workout routine, a new diet, and a rigid work schedule. However, the pressure to do everything perfectly left her feeling overwhelmed and exhausted. After speaking with a therapist, Mia realized that building resilience would require more sustainable, consistent efforts rather than intense bursts of activity. She shifted her focus to small, manageable goals: a 30-minute walk each day, a consistent sleep schedule, and taking regular breaks to rest and recharge. Over time, these small actions added up, and Mia noticed a significant improvement in her energy levels, mood, and overall well-being.

Building resilience through consistency also means developing emotional resilience—the ability to bounce back from setbacks without resorting to old patterns of behavior. It's about accepting that recovery is a gradual process and that healing requires patience. For high achievers, learning to embrace consistency over intensity can be one of the most powerful shifts in their recovery journey.

Conclusion

Rewiring the brain's reward system is a critical component of recovery for high achievers. The process involves replacing unhealthy substances and behaviors with healthy sources of reward—activities that trigger the brain's dopamine system in ways that support long-term well-being. Exercise, creativity, and social connection are powerful tools for achieving this, as they offer sustainable, positive reinforcement that promotes emotional and physical health.

Building resilience through consistency, rather than intensity, allows individuals to create lasting changes that support their recovery journey. By focusing on small, manageable steps and embracing the process of healing, high achievers can rewire their reward system, creating new pathways for pleasure, fulfillment, and growth. Recovery is not about perfection; it's about creating balance, nurturing well-being, and learning to find joy in the small, consistent steps that lead to lasting change.

Chapter 10

Relationships, Roles, and Rebuilding Trust

Introduction

Recovery is a deeply personal journey, one that often requires individuals to confront not only their internal struggles but also the external consequences of their actions on those around them. Whether it's a partner, family member, colleague, or friend, addiction, burnout, or mental health issues can leave emotional scars that affect relationships in profound ways. For high achievers, these struggles are often compounded by the need to maintain a strong image of control and success, which can make it difficult to acknowledge the impact of their behaviors on others.

Rebuilding trust, mending broken relationships, and navigating new dynamics in personal and professional roles are some of the most challenging aspects of recovery. The guilt of past actions, combined with the desire to move forward and heal, can create a complex emotional landscape that requires careful, compassionate work. This chapter will explore how individuals can reconnect with partners, friends, children, and colleagues after recovery begins, addressing the feelings of guilt and grace that come with mending what has been broken. Additionally, we will explore the importance of boundaries and communication in maintaining healthy relationships during and after the recovery process.

Reconnecting with Partners, Friends, Kids, and Colleagues

When a high achiever embarks on the recovery journey, the impact on their relationships is often one of the most significant aspects to consider. Whether it's a partner who has endured years of emotional distance, a child who has been neglected, or a colleague who has witnessed erratic behavior, rebuilding these connections requires vulnerability, empathy, and patience. For many, the damage done to relationships can feel insurmountable, but with consistent effort and honesty, healing is possible.

Reconnecting with Partners

For many individuals in recovery, their relationship with their partner may be the most affected. Partners often bear the brunt of the emotional toll caused by addiction, burnout, or mental health struggles. They may have felt neglected, betrayed, or even gaslit as their partner's behavior spiraled. For high achievers who often hide their struggles behind a façade of success, their partner's sense of abandonment or hurt may have been intensified.

Take the example of John and Sarah. John was a successful CEO who had spent years neglecting his marriage in favor of his career. His intense work schedule, combined with his struggles with alcohol, had strained their relationship to the breaking point. When John entered recovery, he quickly realized that his actions had not only caused damage to his health but had also deeply hurt his wife. Sarah, despite her love for him, had begun to question whether she could trust John again.

The road to rebuilding their relationship was not easy. John knew that he had to take full responsibility for his actions, and Sarah had to be willing to confront her own feelings of betrayal and disappointment. For John, this meant being vulnerable and honest about his struggles, acknowledging the pain he had caused, and showing a consistent commitment to change. For Sarah, it meant finding the courage to forgive, letting go of some of the resentment, and opening herself to the possibility of rebuilding trust.

Over time, John and Sarah began to reconnect through open communication, shared experiences, and a renewed commitment to their relationship. John made a conscious effort to spend quality time with Sarah, listening to her needs, and being present in ways he had not been before. Sarah, in turn, learned to communicate her feelings without judgment, allowing John to show up as his authentic self. While trust would take time to rebuild, they both knew that the process of recovery required patience and understanding from both sides.

Reconnecting with a partner in recovery requires both individuals to be open to change. It is about acknowledging past hurts, forgiving each other, and rebuilding a foundation of mutual respect and trust. For high achievers, learning to balance their personal and professional lives is crucial to ensuring that their recovery does not continue to take a backseat to career ambitions.

Reconnecting with Friends

Friendships are often one of the first things to suffer when an individual is caught in the grips of addiction, burnout, or mental health struggles. High achievers, especially those driven by the need for success, may isolate themselves from friends in favor of working or focusing on their personal issues. Over time, this isolation can create distance, leading to feelings of abandonment and betrayal in the friend group.

For example, Maria, a successful entrepreneur, had spent years neglecting her friendships due to her overwhelming work schedule. As her stress and anxiety grew, she withdrew even further, unable to make time for social events or meaningful conversations. When she entered recovery, she realized that her friendships had deteriorated, and many of her friends had begun to pull away, unsure of how to support her or what to say.

Rebuilding these friendships requires vulnerability and honest communication. Maria had to reach out to her friends, acknowledge her past behavior, and express a genuine desire to reconnect. It was not easy—some friends had been hurt by her absence and didn't know how to approach her recovery. Maria had to be patient, understanding that rebuilding these connections would take time and effort.

For those in recovery, reconnecting with friends often involves a process of rebuilding trust. It is important to show up consistently, be reliable, and demonstrate that the individual is committed to making positive changes. At the same time, it is crucial to be understanding if some friends are hesitant or reluctant to reengage. They may have their own healing process to go through, and rushing them may push them further away.

Reconnecting with Kids

For those in recovery, reconnecting with children can be one of the most emotionally charged aspects of the journey. Children may have witnessed their parent's struggles firsthand, and the impact on their emotional well-being can be significant. Whether it's a father who has been absent due to addiction or a mother who has been emotionally distant due to burnout, children may feel confused, neglected, or betrayed.

Take the example of David, a former executive who had neglected his relationship with his teenage daughter, Emma, due to his alcohol addiction. Emma had spent years feeling overlooked and unheard, and by the time David entered recovery, their relationship had become strained. David realized that reconnecting with Emma would require more than just an apology—it would require building a new foundation based on trust, communication, and emotional availability.

For David, this meant spending quality time with Emma, being present for her emotional needs, and showing her that he was committed to being a better father. He worked to establish open communication with her, allowing her to express her feelings without judgment. Emma, in turn, had to learn to trust her father again, a process that would take time. Through consistent effort and patience, David and Emma slowly rebuilt their bond, learning to communicate more openly and strengthen their relationship.

For parents in recovery, reconnecting with children requires understanding the emotional impact of their actions and being willing to put in the effort to regain trust. It's about showing up, being vulnerable, and allowing the child to see the commitment to change. Recovery can be an opportunity for healing not only for the individual but also for the family unit as a whole.

Reconnecting with Colleagues

In the professional world, relationships with colleagues are often affected by the stress, pressure, and burnout that high achievers face. Colleagues may have witnessed erratic behavior, missed deadlines, or a lack of engagement. In recovery, high performers may face the challenge of rebuilding professional relationships and regaining the trust of their team members.

Take the example of Emily, a senior manager at a global corporation. Emily had always been known for her sharp intellect and work ethic, but over time, the demands of her job began to take a toll on her health. As she struggled with anxiety and burnout, her performance at work began to suffer, leading to tension with her colleagues. When Emily entered recovery, she realized that regaining her professional reputation and relationships would require more than just improving her work performance—it would require rebuilding trust.

For Emily, this meant having open, honest conversations with her colleagues. She took the time to apologize for her past behavior, acknowledging the impact her struggles had on the team. Emily also made a commitment to prioritize her well-being, ensuring that she would not fall back into the same patterns of stress and burnout. Her colleagues, in turn, appreciated her transparency and commitment to change. Over time, Emily was able to rebuild her relationships with her team, not by achieving perfection but by showing up consistently and demonstrating her dedication to growth.

The Guilt and Grace of Mending What's Been Broken

The process of rebuilding relationships after recovery is often accompanied by feelings of guilt. High achievers are typically driven by a strong sense of responsibility, and the idea that their actions have hurt others can be deeply painful. Guilt can feel like an insurmountable weight—a constant reminder of the damage done and the emotional toll that has been placed on loved ones and colleagues.

However, guilt must be understood not as a permanent fixture but as a signal that the individual is aware of the harm caused and is motivated to make amends. Guilt can be a powerful catalyst for change, but when it becomes overwhelming or self-flagellating, it can prevent recovery from progressing. The key is to acknowledge the guilt, make amends where necessary, and then allow grace to play a role in the healing process.

Grace, in the context of recovery, is the ability to forgive oneself and others. It's the recognition that everyone makes mistakes, and the process of healing involves both self-compassion and compassion for others. In the case of John and Sarah, while John felt immense guilt for the years he had neglected his wife, Sarah, through her own healing, was able to offer him grace. She understood that recovery was a journey, and she made the choice to forgive and support him as he worked to rebuild their relationship. This grace allowed both of them to move forward without being trapped in the past.

Boundaries and Communication After Recovery Begins

One of the most important aspects of rebuilding relationships after recovery is establishing and maintaining healthy boundaries. For many high achievers, the lack of boundaries—whether personal or professional—was a significant contributor to their struggles. The pressure to overperform, to please others, and to constantly give of oneself without taking time to recharge can lead to burnout, resentment, and unhealthy relationship dynamics.

In recovery, setting and respecting boundaries becomes an essential practice. Boundaries are not about shutting others out—they are about creating space for self-care, emotional well-being, and mutual respect. For those in recovery, it is crucial to communicate clearly about boundaries, whether it's with a partner, family member, colleague, or friend. Establishing boundaries ensures that individuals can prioritize their needs without feeling guilty or overburdened.

Take the example of Olivia, who, after recovering from burnout, realized that she had to set boundaries in both her personal and professional life. In her marriage, Olivia began to communicate more openly with her husband about her needs for rest and personal time. In her career, she learned to say no to excessive work demands, ensuring that she didn't sacrifice her health or well-being for the sake of success.

These boundaries helped Olivia maintain balance in her relationships and in her recovery journey.

Conclusion

Rebuilding relationships, roles, and trust after recovery is a challenging but deeply rewarding process. For high achievers, the damage caused by addiction, burnout, or mental health struggles can feel insurmountable, but with time, patience, and commitment, healing is possible. By reconnecting with partners, friends, children, and colleagues through vulnerability, empathy, and open communication, individuals can rebuild the foundation of trust that supports long-term recovery. The guilt of past mistakes must be acknowledged but not allowed to define the recovery process. Instead, grace, forgiveness, and healthy boundaries can help foster healing in relationships, leading to stronger connections, greater emotional well-being, and a renewed sense of purpose. Rebuilding trust takes time, but through consistent effort, high achievers can repair what has been broken and create new, healthier patterns in their personal and professional lives.

Chapter 11

Work Without the Numbness

Introduction

For high achievers, work has often been synonymous with identity. It's where success is measured, where personal value is confirmed, and where the sense of accomplishment is most deeply felt. Many professionals, especially those with an intense drive to succeed, fall into the trap of using work as a way to escape the emotional pain, stress, or uncertainty that they may face in their personal lives. This relentless drive can be particularly dangerous when paired with substances—be it caffeine, alcohol, or stimulants—used as fuel to push through exhaustion, dull the emotional edges of burnout, or help manage anxiety.

However, recovery challenges the notion of working while numbed, whether through substances or unhealthy work patterns. The journey of sobriety or emotional healing requires the individual to step into work without relying on substances or unhealthy coping mechanisms. But how does one approach work when the very thing that once made it tolerable—the numbing agent of external highs or unhealthy productivity—has been removed?

This chapter explores how to redefine ambition in a sober life, how to find purpose beyond productivity, and how to stay sharp and focused at work without relying on substances as fuel. By reconnecting with deeper motivations, shifting the focus from mere achievement to meaningful impact, and cultivating healthy work habits, high achievers can work without the numbness that once defined their professional lives. This process not only leads to a more sustainable approach to success but also ensures that work becomes a tool for personal growth and fulfillment, rather than a means of escape.

Redefining Ambition in a Sober Life

Ambition is often seen as the driving force behind success, a key attribute that pushes individuals to achieve extraordinary things. For many high achievers, ambition is their fuel. It's the desire to achieve more, to surpass limits, and to constantly grow. However, in recovery, ambition can become a complicated and dangerous concept. The very ambition that fueled their previous successes may also be the source of their struggles. For some, ambition has been closely tied to external validation—whether that comes in the form of accolades, money, or recognition. For others, it has been tied to a sense of worth, as if their value was determined by their ability to achieve more and more.

The process of recovery requires redefining ambition—moving away from an external, result-driven mindset to a more internal, purpose-driven one. It involves shifting the focus from achieving for the sake of achievement to working in alignment with one's true values and passions.

Take the example of Lisa, a top-performing sales executive in a global tech company. For years, Lisa's ambition had been the driving force behind her success. She worked tirelessly, often using stimulants to fuel her long hours. However, after experiencing a personal breakdown, Lisa realized that her ambition was out of alignment with her values. Her pursuit of success had been motivated by external validation, not by a genuine desire to contribute or create meaningful impact.

In her recovery, Lisa began to redefine her ambition. Instead of measuring success by the number of deals closed or the commissions earned, she began to focus on how she could add value to her company and her clients. She shifted her ambition from personal achievement to creating positive change in the lives of others. By aligning her ambition with her purpose, Lisa not only found greater satisfaction in her work but also created a healthier relationship with it—one that didn't rely on external validation or unhealthy coping mechanisms.

Redefining ambition in a sober life is about asking deeper questions: What drives me beyond external success? What impact do I want to make? How can my work contribute to something larger than myself? By shifting ambition from external metrics to internal fulfillment and purpose, individuals in recovery can create sustainable success without falling into the same unhealthy patterns.

Finding Purpose Beyond Productivity

In a world that often equates productivity with worth, high achievers can easily become trapped in the belief that their value lies in their ability to produce results. This is especially true for those who have used work as a means to escape emotional pain or find validation. The focus on productivity—getting more done, faster, and better—becomes all-consuming, leaving little room for introspection, rest, or enjoyment.

Recovery offers an opportunity to reevaluate what work truly means. The key to maintaining a fulfilling and sustainable career is finding purpose beyond the relentless drive for productivity. This doesn't mean abandoning hard work or ambition; it means shifting the focus from mere output to impact, purpose, and well-being.

John, a successful architect, spent years measuring his success by how many projects he completed and how many clients he satisfied. He equated his worth with his output, believing that the more he achieved, the more valuable he became. However, when John entered recovery, he realized that his drive for productivity had come at the expense of his personal life, mental health, and relationships. He began to ask himself: What was the purpose behind all this work? What did he want his legacy to be?

As John reflected on his career, he realized that the true purpose of his work wasn't to complete as many projects as possible. It was to create spaces that improved people's lives and contributed to communities in meaningful ways. This shift in perspective allowed John to let go of the constant pressure to produce and instead focus on projects that aligned with his deeper values. He became more selective about the work he took on, choosing to focus on projects that had a positive social impact. By reconnecting with the purpose behind his work, John found a renewed sense of fulfillment and meaning in his career.

Finding purpose beyond productivity means asking yourself why you do the work you do. What motivates you beyond deadlines and deliverables? How can you make a difference, no matter how small?

When work is aligned with purpose, it becomes a source of personal fulfillment rather than just a means to an end. This shift allows individuals in recovery to engage in work that nourishes their soul and contributes to their well-being.

Staying Sharp Without Using Substances as Fuel

For many high achievers, substances like caffeine, alcohol, or even prescription medications have become go-to tools for maintaining focus, staying awake, and pushing through exhaustion. These substances provide a temporary boost of energy or clarity, but they come with significant consequences—whether it's physical burnout, mental fatigue, or emotional instability. In recovery, one of the most significant challenges is learning to stay sharp and focused without relying on substances.

The key to staying sharp in recovery is understanding that true mental clarity and focus come from sustainable habits, not quick fixes. This requires building a routine that supports cognitive function, energy levels, and emotional stability. It also means embracing a new definition of productivity—one that prioritizes balance, well-being, and consistent effort rather than intensity or extremes.

For example, Matt, a top-tier lawyer, had relied heavily on caffeine and energy drinks to power through long hours at work. When he entered recovery for anxiety and burnout, he found himself struggling with maintaining focus and energy without the crutches of stimulants. Initially, Matt felt sluggish and distracted, but he soon realized that his previous reliance on substances had sabotaged his natural energy levels and cognitive function.

In recovery, Matt began to implement healthier habits to support his mental sharpness. He started by incorporating regular exercise into his routine—something he had neglected in the past. Physical activity increased his energy levels and helped him clear his mind, making it easier to focus at work. He also adopted a more consistent sleep schedule, ensuring that he was well-rested and alert during the day. By nourishing his body with the proper nutrients, sleep, and physical activity, Matt found that he could stay sharp and focused without the need for caffeine or other substances.

Staying sharp without substances also means developing mental resilience. For those in recovery, resilience comes from consistency and gradual progress rather than quick fixes or bursts of intensity. Mindfulness practices, meditation, and cognitive exercises can help sharpen focus and reduce stress, providing a natural way to stay alert and present without relying on substances. The goal is to build a mental framework that supports clarity, creativity, and concentration while fostering long-term well-being.

Creating Sustainable Work Habits in Recovery

The process of staying sharp without substances or unhealthy coping mechanisms requires the cultivation of sustainable work habits. For many high achievers, the temptation to overwork, push through fatigue, or chase perfection can be overwhelming. However, recovery teaches that sustainable work habits are built on balance, self-care, and consistent effort over time, rather than on extreme bursts of productivity.

One important aspect of creating sustainable work habits is learning to set boundaries. High achievers often struggle with saying no, believing that every opportunity or task is a reflection of their value. In recovery, it's essential to recognize that not every task needs to be taken on, and that saying no is not a sign of failure but an act of self-preservation. By setting clear boundaries and prioritizing what truly matters, individuals can avoid the burnout that often results from overcommitment.

Another key aspect of sustainable work habits is managing stress effectively. Chronic stress is a major contributor to burnout, and in recovery, it's important to develop strategies to manage stress without resorting to substances. This might include taking regular breaks, practicing deep breathing or meditation, or engaging in physical activity. Stress management becomes an ongoing practice, helping individuals maintain their focus and energy throughout the day without the need for external stimulation.

Conclusion

Working without the numbness is one of the most empowering and transformative aspects of recovery. By redefining ambition, finding purpose beyond productivity, and building sustainable work habits, high achievers can approach their careers in a way that supports their long-term well-being and success. Recovery provides the opportunity to step away from the unhealthy cycles of substance use, burnout, and stress, and instead embrace a more balanced, purpose-driven approach to work.

The process of staying sharp without relying on substances involves developing new routines and strategies—ones that prioritize physical health, emotional stability, and mental clarity. By engaging in regular exercise, cultivating creativity, and building strong social connections, individuals can hack their dopamine system and experience natural highs that support their professional lives.

Ultimately, work in recovery becomes an opportunity to contribute meaningfully to others, to grow both personally and professionally, and to create a life that is fulfilling without sacrificing health or happiness. Through consistency, purpose, and balance, individuals can work without the numbness and create sustainable success in all aspects of their lives.

Chapter 12

Cravings, Triggers, and Stress Cycles

Introduction

The journey of recovery is not linear. For high achievers, this journey can be even more complicated by the pressures of professional success, personal expectations, and the constant demands of life. One of the greatest challenges faced by anyone recovering from addiction, burnout, or mental health struggles is the battle with cravings, triggers, and the deep-seated stress cycles that can easily pull an individual back into old habits. For many, these cycles are deeply ingrained—patterns of stress, craving, and relief that have been formed over months or even years of using substances or unhealthy behaviors as coping mechanisms.

Understanding your unique stress-addiction loop is crucial to breaking free from these patterns. Cravings, in particular, can feel like an uncontrollable force, driving individuals to seek relief from emotional or physical pain. The key to overcoming this cycle is not simply resisting the craving or avoiding the trigger, but rather understanding why these urges exist in the first place and how to rewire the brain to respond differently. In this chapter, we will dive into how high achievers can recognize their stress-addiction loops, understand the mental and environmental cues that lead to relapse, and build practical, professional-friendly coping tools to navigate these challenges without falling back into destructive patterns.

Understanding Your Unique Stress-Addiction Loop

At the core of addiction and unhealthy behavior patterns is the stress-addiction loop. This loop begins when a person experiences stress—whether it's work-related, personal, or emotional. The stress is often accompanied by feelings of discomfort, anxiety, or overwhelm, which then triggers the desire to seek relief. For many, substances or unhealthy behaviors such as overeating, alcohol, gambling, or excessive work provide an escape from this discomfort. The brain, in turn, associates these behaviors with stress relief, reinforcing the behavior over time. This creates a cycle in which the individual becomes dependent on these substances or behaviors to manage stress.

Take the example of Mark, a successful entrepreneur who had spent years building his business. Mark's high levels of stress, combined with his tendency to overwork, led him to develop a pattern of using alcohol to unwind after long days. At first, a drink or two provided relief from the stress of running a company, but over time, the alcohol became an automatic response to stress. The more stressed Mark became, the more he relied on alcohol to calm his nerves. This cycle became increasingly difficult to break, even when Mark began his recovery journey.

Mark's stress-addiction loop was tied to a specific trigger: after intense meetings or long workdays, he would feel a surge of stress that created a craving for alcohol. His brain had associated the two—stress and alcohol—so strongly that breaking the loop felt nearly impossible. Understanding this loop was the first step in Mark's recovery. He needed to identify the triggers that set off his cravings and develop healthier ways to manage stress without relying on substances.

The stress-addiction loop is not limited to substances like alcohol or drugs—it can also manifest in unhealthy behaviors like overworking, compulsive eating, or emotional numbing through social media or television. High achievers are particularly vulnerable to this loop because they often use work, achievement, or external validation as a means to cope with stress. Understanding that this cycle exists is crucial, as it allows individuals to begin to make conscious decisions to break the cycle before it spirals into destructive behaviors.

Mental and Environmental Cues That Lead to Relapse

Relapse is often triggered by specific mental and environmental cues—situations or feelings that bring up old patterns of behavior. These cues can range from stressors at work to personal relationship issues, and they often lead to cravings or urges to revert to old coping mechanisms. Understanding the mental and environmental cues that lead to relapse is key to managing them and ultimately breaking the stress-addiction cycle.

Mental Cues: Emotional Triggers and Thought Patterns

Mental cues are often internal, stemming from emotional states, thoughts, or unresolved issues. For high achievers, the pressure to perform, perfectionism, and fear of failure can create intense emotional distress. These feelings can trigger cravings for the temporary relief substances or unhealthy behaviors once provided.

Consider the example of Sarah, a high-level marketing executive who had struggled with workaholism. Sarah had long used work as a way to avoid dealing with anxiety and self-doubt. Whenever she felt overwhelmed or uncertain about her abilities, she would throw herself into her work, pushing through exhaustion to avoid confronting her emotional discomfort. Over time, this developed into a pattern—whenever Sarah faced feelings of anxiety, inadequacy, or fear of failure, she would turn to work to numb those emotions.

When Sarah entered recovery, she had to confront the underlying mental cues that triggered her workaholism. She began to identify the emotional triggers that led her to overwork, such as feelings of imposter syndrome, fear of failure, or perfectionism. By recognizing these emotional patterns, Sarah was able to create healthier coping mechanisms—such as mindfulness, therapy, and self-compassion—that allowed her to manage her anxiety without resorting to the same numbing behaviors.

Mental cues are often linked to deeply ingrained thought patterns. For example, the belief that "I'm not good enough unless I'm perfect" or "I need to keep pushing to avoid failure" can create a constant cycle of stress and anxiety. These thoughts, in turn, lead to cravings for substances or behaviors that offer immediate relief, but do not address the underlying emotional issue. In recovery, it is essential to recognize these mental cues and challenge them. Cognitive-behavioral techniques (CBT) are often effective in breaking these thought patterns, allowing individuals to reframe their thinking and develop healthier emotional responses to stress.

Environmental Cues: Work, Social, and Physical Triggers

Environmental cues are external factors—people, places, situations, or even physical locations—that can trigger cravings and relapse. For high achievers, certain environments may be particularly triggering, such as high-stress work settings, social situations where alcohol or substances are present, or even specific routines or locations associated with old habits.

Take, for example, Jason, a successful finance executive who had struggled with alcohol addiction. Jason's environment was often filled with work-related stress, late-night meetings, and social events where drinking was a key part of the culture. During recovery, Jason realized that many of his relapses were triggered by being in specific environments—like after a tense meeting or at a company event—where alcohol was readily available. These situations created a mental and emotional link to drinking, making it difficult for him to resist the urge to relapse.

One of the most important steps in breaking free from environmental cues is changing the environments that trigger cravings. For Jason, this meant setting boundaries with work events and social gatherings. He started avoiding situations where alcohol was the primary focus and instead chose to engage in activities that did not involve substances. He also worked with his colleagues and superiors to create a healthier work environment that reduced stress and allowed for more meaningful, supportive interactions.

In addition to changing social and work-related environments, individuals in recovery should also address physical cues. For example, if a person's home or office is associated with substance use or unhealthy behavior, it may be necessary to make changes to the physical space. This could involve clearing out old substances, creating a calming, supportive environment, or even rearranging the space to create positive associations. Making these physical changes helps reduce the triggers that prompt cravings and provides a more supportive environment for recovery.

Building Practical, Professional-Friendly Coping Tools

One of the greatest challenges for high achievers in recovery is learning how to cope with stress, cravings, and triggers in a way that aligns with their professional and personal responsibilities. High achievers often operate in high-pressure environments where performance is closely tied to identity, and the ability to cope with stress is a crucial skill. The key to managing cravings and triggers in a professional setting is building coping tools that are both effective and sustainable.

1. Mindfulness and Meditation

Mindfulness and meditation are powerful tools for managing stress and cravings in a professional setting. These practices involve focusing on the present moment without judgment and cultivating awareness of one's thoughts, feelings, and physical sensations. For high achievers, mindfulness offers a way to break the stress-addiction loop by teaching them to observe cravings and emotional responses without reacting to them impulsively.

For example, during stressful meetings or workdays, an individual in recovery can practice mindfulness by taking short breaks to focus on their breath, bringing their attention back to the present moment. Mindfulness helps interrupt the automatic reaction to stress and cravings, allowing the individual to respond more thoughtfully rather than being swept away by old patterns.

In addition to mindfulness, meditation provides a structured practice for cultivating calm and focus. Taking just five to ten minutes each day for meditation can reduce anxiety, improve concentration, and help individuals stay grounded in moments of stress.

2. Physical Activity and Exercise

Exercise is another powerful coping tool that can help manage stress and reduce cravings. Physical activity triggers the release of dopamine and endorphins, providing a natural, healthy high that can replace the need for substances. For high achievers, exercise can also provide a way to manage the physical symptoms of stress, such as tension, fatigue, or restlessness.

Incorporating regular physical activity into one's routine—whether it's yoga, running, swimming, or strength training—offers a way to stay sharp, energized, and focused. Exercise not only helps with cravings but also improves sleep, boosts mood, and reduces the risk of burnout.

3. Building a Support Network

Having a strong support network is essential in recovery. For high achievers, this means surrounding themselves with individuals who understand their struggles, offer encouragement, and hold them accountable. Whether it's a therapist, a support group, or trusted friends and colleagues, having people to talk to during moments of stress and craving can make all the difference.

Support groups, both in-person and online, offer a safe space to share experiences, discuss challenges, and receive advice from others who are going through similar struggles. For professionals, finding a network of people who understand the unique challenges of balancing recovery with high-pressure work can be especially beneficial.

4. Time Management and Setting Boundaries

High achievers often struggle with overcommitment, which can contribute to stress and cravings. Learning to manage time effectively and set boundaries is crucial for maintaining long-term recovery. This means learning to say no when necessary, prioritizing self-care, and ensuring that work and personal life are balanced.

For example, an individual in recovery might set specific work hours and avoid checking emails or taking work calls after hours. They may also schedule regular breaks during the day to relax and recharge, ensuring that their workload doesn't lead to burnout or emotional exhaustion. Setting these boundaries creates space for recovery and helps manage stress before it becomes overwhelming.

Conclusion

Understanding cravings, triggers, and stress cycles is essential for breaking the patterns of addiction, burnout, or unhealthy behavior that many high achievers face. By recognizing the unique stress-addiction loops, identifying mental and environmental cues, and building practical coping tools, individuals can begin to regain control over their responses to stress and cravings. Recovery is not just about abstaining from substances or unhealthy behaviors—it's about creating a sustainable, balanced lifestyle that promotes emotional well-being, resilience, and long-term success.

For high achievers in recovery, the journey is about more than just overcoming cravings—it's about transforming how they approach stress, work, and personal fulfillment. By developing mindfulness, exercising regularly, building a support network, and setting boundaries, individuals can navigate cravings and triggers with grace and consistency. Ultimately, the goal is to break free from the stress-addiction loop and build a life that is grounded in health, purpose, and sustainable success.

Chapter 13

Staying Sober in High-Stakes Environments

Introduction

For high achievers, the pressures of their professional and personal lives can create an environment where substance use—whether it's alcohol, stimulants, or other coping mechanisms—feels like a necessary crutch. Success-driven individuals often navigate high-stakes environments, from dealing with demanding clients to attending social events where alcohol flows freely, working late nights under tight deadlines, and experiencing a constant barrage of pressure to perform. In these settings, the temptation to revert to old habits can feel overwhelming. Staying sober in these environments requires more than just willpower; it requires a strategic approach, grounded in personal boundaries, self-awareness, and a commitment to living a healthier, more sustainable life.

In this chapter, we will explore how high achievers can maintain their sobriety while facing the pressures of clients, events, late nights, and high expectations. We will discuss practical strategies for saying "no" with power and poise, navigating situations where sobriety might be challenged, and how to create or find sober-friendly spaces that support long-term recovery and professional success.

Dealing with Clients, Events, Late Nights, and Pressure

The professional world, especially for high achievers, can often feel like a never-ending cycle of high-stakes situations, tight deadlines, and high-pressure decisions. For many professionals, the pressure to meet these demands leads to unhealthy coping mechanisms—substances like alcohol or caffeine, or workaholism—used to alleviate stress or enhance performance. However, when individuals decide to pursue recovery, navigating these high-pressure environments without reverting to old habits can seem daunting.

Managing Clients and High-Pressure Work Relationships

In business and client-facing roles, the pressure to perform is often immense. Whether it's securing a deal, finalizing a project, or meeting an impossible deadline, the stakes can feel high. These situations frequently lead to stress, and for those in recovery, the urge to turn to substances as a form of relief can be particularly strong.

Take the example of Lily, a senior account manager at a marketing firm. Lily's job required her to work long hours, attend networking events, and entertain high-profile clients. She used to rely on alcohol to unwind after high-pressure meetings, believing that it helped her relax and bond with clients. However, after entering recovery, Lily realized that alcohol was no longer a tool for connection—it was a crutch that enabled unhealthy behavior and kept her stuck in a cycle of numbing rather than addressing the stress head-on.

For Lily, the key to staying sober while managing high-pressure client relationships was learning to create healthier ways of coping. Rather than turning to alcohol during a stressful meeting, she began practicing mindfulness techniques, taking short walks to reset her mind, and using breathing exercises to manage her anxiety. She also began to communicate more openly with her clients about her personal commitment to living a healthier lifestyle, which allowed her to set expectations and boundaries without fear of judgment.

For high achievers like Lily, staying sober in client-facing roles requires a proactive approach to stress management. It's about building healthier relationships with clients that don't revolve around substances. This might mean adjusting the way meetings are structured—choosing a morning coffee instead of a cocktail hour, for instance—or setting clear expectations for what is and isn't acceptable in professional environments. Clients often appreciate professionalism, and sobriety can be an asset that contributes to clear-headed decision-making and long-term success.

Navigating Events and Social Situations

High-achieving professionals often find themselves attending networking events, conferences, or industry gatherings where alcohol is prevalent. These events can be particularly challenging for those in recovery, as they may feel socially pressured to partake in drinking or drug use as a way to fit in or feel "normal." The fear of judgment, the desire to avoid awkwardness, or the need to "blend in" can make maintaining sobriety in these situations feel impossible.

For example, David, a successful consultant, often attended business dinners and social networking events where alcohol was a central element of the evening. Early in his recovery, he struggled with feelings of isolation and discomfort when he was the only person at the table not drinking. However, he realized that his decision to stay sober didn't need to be a source of shame—it could actually be a point of strength and self-assurance.

David began practicing how to gracefully decline a drink. Instead of focusing on the pressure to conform, he started viewing these events as opportunities to build authentic connections based on mutual respect and shared interests—not just based on drinking or socializing to excess. David would bring up his commitment to sobriety when relevant, and if anyone questioned it, he would calmly explain his personal journey without feeling the need to justify himself.

In these environments, it's crucial to have a set of strategies to navigate the social pressure that can arise. Some practical tips include:

- **Plan Ahead**: Before attending an event, make a clear decision about what you're comfortable with. Whether it's deciding not to drink at all or setting a time limit for how long you'll stay at the event, having a plan in place can reduce stress and increase confidence.

- **Have a Non-Alcoholic Drink in Hand**: Holding a drink—even if it's just water, soda, or a mocktail—can help you avoid being offered alcohol and make you feel less conspicuous.

- **Set Boundaries Early**: If the social pressure becomes overwhelming, it's okay to set a boundary. Excuse yourself from uncomfortable situations, leave early if necessary, or even politely tell people that you don't drink anymore. Over time, the more you practice setting these boundaries, the easier it becomes.

- **Find Like-minded Individuals**: At many events, there are others who share your commitment to sobriety or are just looking for deeper, more meaningful connections. It can help to seek out those people who are interested in conversations beyond the typical alcohol-driven chatter.

Ultimately, staying sober at social events is about creating a new relationship with socializing—one that doesn't rely on substances for connection or relaxation. It's about learning to have fun, make genuine connections, and enjoy the experience without the need to numb or escape.

Late Nights and High-Stress Situations

In many high-stakes environments, late nights are inevitable. Whether it's working on a tight deadline, attending an all-night networking event, or simply trying to finish a project, late nights are a common part of the professional life of a high achiever. For those in recovery, these long hours can pose a challenge, especially if the late-night work culture previously involved substance use or unhealthy coping mechanisms to stay alert or calm.

Maria, a senior executive at a technology firm, found that late nights often triggered cravings for alcohol or caffeine. The stress of her job, combined with the fatigue of working long hours, made her more susceptible to the temptation to turn to substances to stay alert or relax. However, Maria realized that relying on substances for late-night productivity wasn't sustainable and often led to burnout. She started experimenting with healthier strategies to stay sharp during late nights, such as drinking herbal teas, taking short breaks to stretch, and setting clear limits on how late she would work.

For high achievers, it's important to acknowledge that working late doesn't have to be synonymous with burnout or reliance on substances. There are effective strategies to manage late-night work while maintaining sobriety:

- **Prioritize Rest**: Even during busy times, it's important to prioritize rest and recovery. This means scheduling breaks, taking naps when possible, and getting enough sleep to maintain energy levels.

- **Eat for Sustained Energy**: Foods that provide slow-releasing energy, such as whole grains, lean proteins, and fruits, can help sustain focus during late-night work without the need for caffeine or stimulants.

- **Use Natural Focus Tools**: Practices like mindfulness, breathing exercises, or even light stretching can help reenergize your mind and body during late nights, keeping you focused and clear-headed.

Saying "No" with Power and Poise

One of the most powerful tools in staying sober in high-stakes environments is the ability to say "no." High achievers often face an overwhelming number of requests, opportunities, and expectations. Learning to say no without guilt or feeling like you're missing out is crucial to maintaining a healthy, sober lifestyle.

Saying no can feel difficult, especially for high achievers who are used to saying yes to everything. However, it is essential for maintaining boundaries, reducing stress, and preventing burnout. Saying no is not a sign of weakness; rather, it is a sign of strength and self-awareness. It is about protecting your time, energy, and well-being.

The Power of Saying No

Take the example of Jonathan, a senior lawyer at a prestigious law firm. Jonathan was known for his exceptional work ethic, but this often meant he took on more than he could handle. His fear of disappointing others led him to say yes to every request, often working long hours and sacrificing his well-being. When Jonathan entered recovery, he realized that his tendency to overcommit had been a key driver of his stress and burnout. He had to learn to say no in a way that was respectful to others, but firm in his commitment to his own health.

Saying no with power and poise means doing so confidently, without apologizing for your decision. For Jonathan, it meant communicating clearly with colleagues and clients about his priorities, setting realistic expectations, and establishing boundaries that would protect his time and energy. By learning to say no, he was able to maintain better control over his workload and reduce the pressure that had previously contributed to his substance use.

How to Say No Gracefully

- **Be Direct, But Polite**: When you need to say no, be direct and clear, but do so with kindness. You don't have to provide an elaborate explanation; simply stating that you are unable to commit to something due to other priorities can be sufficient.

- **Offer Alternatives**: If appropriate, offer an alternative solution. For example, you might say, "I'm unable to take on this project, but I recommend [name] as someone who can help." This allows you to decline without leaving the other person feeling unsupported.

- **Set Clear Boundaries**: Communicate your boundaries early and often. Let others know when you are available and when you are not. Setting these expectations up front helps reduce the pressure to say yes in the first place.

Finding or Creating Sober-Friendly Spaces

One of the most important aspects of staying sober in high-stakes environments is finding or creating sober-friendly spaces. For high achievers, this means establishing environments—both professionally and personally—that support sobriety and encourage healthy, positive interactions.

- **Professional Sober-Friendly Spaces**: In many industries, the culture can revolve around alcohol, late-night meetings, or stressful work environments. However, it is possible to create or find sober-friendly spaces within these environments. This could include choosing to host meetings in coffee shops instead of bars or creating a company-wide culture that values health and well-being over workaholism and substance use.

- **Social Sober-Friendly Spaces**: When attending social events, seek out or create spaces that don't revolve around alcohol or other substances. This could mean organizing activities that focus on shared interests like fitness, creativity, or community service, where the emphasis is on connection rather than substance use.

- **Personal Sober-Friendly Spaces**: At home or in personal life, it's essential to create spaces where sobriety is supported. This could involve setting up a designated area for relaxation or self-care, making sure that there are no triggers or reminders of past habits.

Conclusion

Staying sober in high-stakes environments requires a combination of strategy, self-awareness, and resilience. By learning to manage pressure, set boundaries, and navigate high-pressure situations with grace, high achievers can maintain their sobriety while thriving professionally. Saying no with power, creating sober-friendly spaces, and building healthier coping mechanisms all contribute to a sustainable path to recovery. Through these strategies, individuals can break free from the cycles of stress and substance use, building a more fulfilling, balanced life where professional success is achieved without compromising health or well-being.

Chapter 14

When You Fall—Relapse and Renewal

Introduction

Relapse is one of the most difficult and emotionally charged aspects of any recovery journey. For high achievers, the stakes are often higher, and the personal cost of relapse can feel catastrophic. The temptation to see relapse as a failure can be overwhelming—especially for individuals who pride themselves on their ability to control their environment, achieve goals, and maintain high standards. However, recovery is rarely a straightforward path, and the reality is that setbacks are part of the process. How we respond to those setbacks, how we learn from them, and how we pick ourselves up after a fall are what ultimately define our success in recovery.

Relapse doesn't mean the end of recovery—it's simply feedback. It's an opportunity to gain deeper insight into the triggers, patterns, and emotions that led to the setback. The way we rebound from relapse—how we handle our guilt, our actions, and our relationship with ourselves—is what determines whether we continue to progress or allow the relapse to spiral into a prolonged setback. In this chapter, we will explore the process of relapse and renewal, discussing how to view relapse as feedback rather than failure, how to rebound with integrity and insight, and how to make peace with imperfection.

Relapse Isn't Failure—It's Feedback

For high achievers, the concept of failure can be anathema. Many of us have spent our entire lives striving for perfection, constantly pushing ourselves to succeed and be the best. We've been conditioned to view success as an indication of our worth and failure as an unacceptable flaw. As a result, when relapse happens—whether it's a slip in sobriety, a return to old stress behaviors, or a moment of emotional breakdown—the tendency is to internalize it as a personal failure.

However, relapse is not a failure. It's feedback. It's an opportunity to evaluate the choices, circumstances, or internal struggles that led to the relapse and to use that information to adjust and grow. Rather than seeing relapse as a setback, it can be viewed as a stepping stone in the recovery journey—something to learn from and build upon.

Take the example of Tom, a senior executive who had been in recovery for six months after a period of alcohol addiction. Tom had made significant progress: his relationships had improved, his stress management techniques were working, and he was feeling healthier both physically and emotionally. However, after a particularly stressful week filled with long meetings and personal issues, Tom found himself at a company event where alcohol was served. Despite his commitment to sobriety, he found himself slipping into old habits and drinking. The next morning, he felt ashamed and devastated, convinced that his recovery was over.

Tom's initial instinct was to label this moment as a failure. However, with support from his therapist and recovery group, he reframed the experience. Instead of viewing it as a complete breakdown, Tom saw it as feedback: he had been under tremendous stress, and his emotional reserves were low. His relapse was a result of a combination of environmental triggers, emotional fatigue, and unaddressed stress. Recognizing these factors allowed him to take action and adjust his recovery plan moving forward. He realized he needed to develop stronger coping mechanisms for stress, learn to recognize when he was emotionally overwhelmed, and create a more robust support system for tough moments.

Relapse provides valuable feedback. It offers an opportunity to reflect on the areas where a person may be vulnerable, the gaps in their coping strategies, or the triggers that lead to old patterns. This insight allows the individual to take proactive steps to address these factors and strengthen their commitment to recovery.

In high-stakes environments, particularly those involving work, family, or social pressures, recognizing relapse as feedback rather than failure can significantly alter the emotional landscape of recovery. It's not about being perfect; it's about making progress, learning from setbacks, and continuing to move forward. This shift in mindset allows individuals to experience the freedom to fail, knowing that every setback is an opportunity to refine and strengthen their recovery process.

How to Rebound with Integrity and Insight

When relapse occurs, it's easy to feel defeated, overwhelmed by guilt, or even shame. Many high achievers struggle with perfectionism and the pressure to maintain an image of unshakable control. As a result, they may avoid acknowledging the relapse, hiding it from themselves or others, which can ultimately exacerbate the problem. Rebounding with integrity means facing the relapse head-on, taking responsibility for it, and using the experience to grow stronger.

Rebounding with integrity involves three key steps: honesty, self-compassion, and action.

1. Honesty with Yourself

The first step in rebounding with integrity is being honest with yourself about what happened. This means resisting the urge to minimize the relapse or make excuses. Honesty is crucial because it allows you to take full responsibility for your actions and decisions. It also enables you to recognize the root causes of the relapse, which is the first step in preventing it from happening again.

For example, when Sarah, a project manager at a leading tech company, relapsed after months of sobriety, she initially found it hard to admit the truth. She had always prided herself on her ability to control her environment and emotions. However, she knew deep down that her relapse was not just about a temporary loss of willpower—it was about a combination of overwhelming work stress, emotional neglect, and a failure to recognize when she needed support. Once she acknowledged these factors, she was able to see her relapse as a learning experience.

Honesty with yourself can be painful, but it's necessary for growth. The act of confronting the relapse directly—without denial or self-deception—gives you the clarity needed to take corrective action.

2. Self-Compassion and Forgiveness

After a relapse, guilt is often the first emotion that surfaces. For high achievers, guilt can feel like a permanent stain on their progress, a sign of personal failure. However, guilt is not a productive emotion; it keeps individuals stuck in a cycle of self-punishment rather than motivating them to change. What's more important than guilt is self-compassion— the ability to forgive yourself and accept that setbacks are part of the recovery process.

Take the example of Rob, a marketing director who had been working through recovery for an eating disorder. After a stressful period at work, Rob found himself returning to unhealthy eating patterns. Initially, Rob was consumed with guilt, believing that he had ruined all the progress he had made. However, after speaking with his therapist, Rob was reminded that recovery is not a linear process. Self-compassion was the key to moving forward. Instead of harshly judging himself, he allowed space for the mistake, recognized the emotional triggers that led to it, and made a commitment to handle the next stress trigger differently.

Self-compassion is essential for maintaining integrity in recovery. Rather than seeing a relapse as a reason to abandon the journey, it is an opportunity to practice forgiveness and self-love. The more compassion you can show yourself, the more likely you are to continue making progress rather than falling back into old patterns of self-doubt or isolation.

3. Action: Making Practical Changes

The final step in rebounding with integrity is taking action. This means using the feedback from the relapse to make meaningful changes in your approach to recovery. Action involves evaluating the circumstances that led to the relapse and finding practical, professional-friendly solutions that address the root causes of the setback.

For Emma, a senior consultant who had been managing anxiety through unhealthy workaholism, her relapse happened during a particularly demanding project. Instead of resigning herself to the idea that work stress was inevitable, Emma made a series of changes: she restructured her schedule to prioritize rest, set clearer boundaries with clients, and sought out additional support from her recovery network. Most importantly, she developed a proactive stress management plan that included mindfulness practices, scheduled breaks, and delegating tasks when necessary.

Rebounding with integrity means taking actionable steps to address vulnerabilities and improve coping mechanisms. It's not about perfection; it's about continuously refining your approach to recovery and building resilience in the face of challenges. Each relapse provides the opportunity to identify areas for improvement and develop new strategies for long-term success.

Making Peace with Imperfection

Recovery, by its very nature, involves imperfection. It requires the acceptance that setbacks, mistakes, and lapses are part of the human experience. High achievers often struggle with the concept of imperfection, as their identity has been shaped by success and achievement. The pressure to perform at the highest level can make even the slightest mistake feel catastrophic. However, making peace with imperfection is a crucial part of long-term recovery.

1. Letting Go of Perfectionism

One of the greatest challenges in recovery for high achievers is letting go of perfectionism. The belief that everything must be flawless can create unrealistic expectations that set individuals up for disappointment. In recovery, the goal is not to achieve perfection, but to make consistent progress. Accepting that relapse is part of the journey allows you to move forward with a sense of peace, knowing that mistakes don't define your worth or success.

For example, James, an executive in a high-pressure job, struggled with perfectionism throughout his recovery. He constantly pushed himself to meet impossible standards, believing that anything less than perfection was failure. When James relapsed, he felt devastated. But through therapy, he began to understand that recovery isn't about achieving perfection—it's about progress. By letting go of his perfectionist tendencies, James learned to accept setbacks without allowing them to derail his entire recovery process.

2. Redefining Success in Recovery

In recovery, success is not about avoiding relapse altogether—it's about developing the resilience to get back on track after a setback.

Success is found in the ability to learn from mistakes, grow from challenges, and continue moving forward with a sense of purpose and commitment. Redefining success in this way allows high achievers to release the pressure of achieving perfection and embrace the messy, imperfect reality of recovery.

For Elizabeth, a successful executive who had battled depression, the pressure to be perfect was overwhelming. After a relapse, Elizabeth realized that her version of success was flawed. Success wasn't about being perfect or never slipping—it was about finding the strength to get back up, to learn, and to keep moving forward. By redefining success, Elizabeth freed herself from the unrealistic expectations that had once held her back.

3. Embracing the Process of Growth

Finally, making peace with imperfection means embracing the process of growth. Recovery is not a destination but a journey—one that involves continual learning, self-discovery, and transformation. Rather than striving for a perfect recovery, the focus should be on the process of becoming better, more resilient, and more self-aware with each passing day.

In recovery, growth comes from the willingness to embrace imperfection, to learn from setbacks, and to keep pushing forward even when the road gets tough. Making peace with imperfection is essential for maintaining long-term progress and avoiding the self-judgment that can keep you stuck.

Conclusion

Relapse is not the end of recovery—it is an opportunity for growth, learning, and renewal. High achievers must learn to view relapse not as failure, but as feedback—a moment to reflect, reassess, and adjust their strategies. Rebounding from relapse with integrity means being honest with yourself, showing self-compassion, and taking practical action to improve your recovery plan. Most importantly, it means making peace with imperfection, letting go of perfectionism, and embracing the process of growth. Recovery is about progress, not perfection, and it is through our setbacks that we learn the most important lessons. By approaching relapse with a mindset of learning and renewal, high achievers can continue to build a stronger, more resilient path toward lasting recovery.

Chapter 15

Sober and Still Sharp

Introduction

For high achievers, the journey of recovery is about more than just abstaining from substances or unhealthy behaviors—it's about rediscovering what success truly means and how to lead a life that is not only sober but also fully engaged, alive, and connected. Many high achievers associate success with external markers: career accomplishments, financial rewards, social status, and professional recognition. However, when recovery begins, this definition of success is often challenged, and individuals are called to redefine it in a way that aligns with their new values, goals, and healthier perspectives on life. The question then becomes: How can someone who has achieved so much in their career find new, sustainable definitions of success that honor their recovery while still keeping them sharp, motivated, and ambitious?

This chapter will explore how high achievers can redefine what success looks like now that they are sober. It will examine how they can become leaders and role models in recovery, using their experiences to inspire others. Lastly, we will discuss how to live fully alive, clear-headed, and connected to the world around you—both in your personal and professional life—without relying on substances or unhealthy habits to fuel success. Being sober doesn't mean losing your edge; in fact, it can sharpen it in ways you never thought possible.

Redefining What Success Looks Like Now

In recovery, one of the most powerful shifts that needs to take place is a reevaluation of what success truly means. For high achievers, success has often been equated with external achievements: a promotion, a pay raise, a prestigious award, or public recognition. However, when the layers of substance use or unhealthy coping mechanisms are peeled back, the question becomes less about external validation and more about internal fulfillment. Success, now, is not measured by how much you can accomplish or how others perceive you but by how well you align with your own values and live in a way that is authentic and sustainable.

Shifting from External Validation to Internal Fulfillment

For years, Matt, a successful entrepreneur, had linked his self-worth to his ability to build and grow his businesses. He thrived on external validation—awards, media recognition, and social praise—but as he entered recovery from alcohol addiction, Matt realized that these markers of success were fleeting and ultimately unsatisfying. He had spent so much of his life chasing approval that he had neglected his personal life, his health, and his emotional well-being.

In recovery, Matt began to redefine what success meant to him. Rather than chasing external validation, he turned inward and started asking himself: What does success look like for me in this moment? How can I measure my life by things that truly matter—like health, peace of mind, connection with family, and alignment with my values? His new definition of success wasn't about how many zeros were in his bank account or how many accolades he received. Instead, it was about creating a life that felt meaningful, fulfilling, and authentic.

For high achievers in recovery, redefining success often involves breaking free from the external metrics that once defined their lives and embracing a more holistic approach. This might mean focusing on personal well-being—physical health, emotional balance, and mental clarity—over work-related success. It might mean nurturing relationships, pursuing meaningful hobbies, or finding a sense of purpose outside of career accomplishments. The goal is not to abandon ambition but to shift the focus from external markers of success to a more balanced and internally fulfilling life.

The Role of Well-Being in Redefining Success

In recovery, true success is found in cultivating well-being. For high achievers, success is no longer about doing more or achieving more at any cost—it's about doing the things that are right for their long-term health and happiness. Well-being is the foundation on which a sustainable version of success is built. This involves integrating practices that support mental, physical, and emotional health—such as regular exercise, healthy eating, mindfulness, therapy, and positive social connections. When well-being is prioritized, success is no longer defined by external achievement alone; it's defined by balance, satisfaction, and inner peace.

Take Maria, a renowned lawyer who spent years chasing promotions and accolades in a cutthroat industry. She was at the top of her field but felt burnt out, disconnected from her own emotions, and distant from her family. When Maria entered recovery, she began to redefine her success in terms of balance rather than ambition. She focused on rebuilding her health, repairing her relationships, and finding ways to work that were fulfilling without sacrificing her personal life. She was no longer chasing an elusive "perfect" version of success but instead embracing a success that was rooted in well-being and sustainable living.

Redefining success in recovery is about creating a life that honors your values, health, and well-being rather than chasing the elusive dream of perfection. It's about finding fulfillment in the journey, not just the destination. The shift in mindset allows individuals to continue achieving in their professional lives while also enjoying a more balanced, rewarding personal life.

Becoming a Leader and Role Model in Recovery

In many cases, high achievers in recovery have the opportunity to become leaders and role models—not just in their professional fields, but in their recovery communities and personal lives. People who have overcome addiction, burnout, or other challenges have a unique perspective that can inspire and guide others through their own struggles. Becoming a leader in recovery doesn't mean perfecting your life; it means using your experiences to show others what is possible when they commit to their health, well-being, and growth.

Leading by Example

One of the most powerful ways high achievers in recovery can lead is by setting an example. By embracing sobriety, setting boundaries, and prioritizing their health, they demonstrate to others that it is possible to thrive without relying on substances or unhealthy coping mechanisms. Leading by example can be particularly powerful in environments where high-pressure and toxic work cultures often encourage unhealthy behaviors, such as overwork, substance use, and emotional neglect.

Consider Jonathan, a highly respected business consultant who had struggled with workaholism and alcohol addiction. As he navigated his recovery, Jonathan realized that his role as a leader in his industry was an opportunity to create change. He began speaking openly about his struggles with addiction and burnout and how recovery had transformed his life. He incorporated discussions about mental health and self-care into his professional relationships and work environment. Over time, Jonathan became a role model not only for his colleagues but also for his clients, showing them that success could be achieved without sacrificing health or happiness.

By sharing their experiences, leaders in recovery can normalize the conversation around mental health, addiction, and the importance of self-care. They can break down the stigma that often surrounds these issues and create an environment where others feel safe seeking help. Leaders who embrace vulnerability and authenticity can inspire others to take their own recovery journeys seriously and offer the support needed to foster collective healing.

Mentorship and Support

Another way that high achievers can become role models in recovery is by becoming mentors. Individuals who have been through the recovery process have a wealth of insight and experience that can help others navigate their own challenges. Mentorship is not about having all the answers; it's about sharing experiences, offering encouragement, and providing a safe space for others to talk about their struggles.

Mentoring others in recovery can be incredibly rewarding. It allows high achievers to use their success, both personal and professional, to guide and uplift others. Mentors can provide practical advice on managing work-life balance, setting boundaries, and maintaining sobriety, as well as offering emotional support for those navigating the ups and downs of recovery. The act of mentoring also reinforces the mentor's own commitment to their journey, making it easier to stay focused and engaged in their personal growth.

Living Fully Alive, Clear, and Connected

For high achievers in recovery, one of the most significant benefits of sobriety is the ability to live fully alive. Substance use, burnout, and unhealthy behaviors often leave individuals feeling numb, disconnected, and unfulfilled. In recovery, individuals have the opportunity to rediscover their passions, reconnect with their values, and live with clarity and purpose.

Clarity of Purpose

One of the most profound gifts of sobriety is the clarity that comes with it. When individuals are no longer relying on substances to numb their emotions or dull their senses, they begin to see their lives with greater clarity. This clarity allows them to align their actions with their values, make decisions that are in line with their true desires, and focus on what truly matters.

For Sarah, a marketing executive who had struggled with workaholism, recovery brought a newfound sense of clarity. As she got sober and developed healthier coping mechanisms, she realized that her career was no longer the only source of fulfillment in her life. She began to pursue hobbies and activities that had once brought her joy, like painting and hiking, and she rekindled her relationships with friends and family. She no longer felt consumed by the need to prove herself through her career but was able to live more authentically, focused on what truly mattered to her.

Living Fully Alive

Sobriety allows individuals to experience life with greater fullness and depth. When individuals are no longer using substances or unhealthy behaviors to escape discomfort, they are able to engage with their emotions, relationships, and experiences more deeply. Living fully alive means embracing all aspects of life—the highs and the lows—and being present for each moment.

For Thomas, a successful architect who had used alcohol to cope with stress, sobriety allowed him to experience life in ways he never had before. He found that his relationships with his family became richer and more meaningful, and he was able to pursue activities that brought him joy, like traveling and learning new skills. Sobriety allowed Thomas to truly engage with life, rather than retreating into a state of numbness.

Living fully alive also means being open to new experiences, new people, and new possibilities. Sobriety often opens doors to personal growth, allowing individuals to explore different paths and live more authentically. It's about embracing a future filled with potential, free from the constraints of old habits and unhealthy behaviors.

Connection with Others

Finally, sobriety allows individuals to forge deeper, more meaningful connections with others. Addiction, burnout, and unhealthy coping mechanisms often lead to isolation and disconnection. In recovery, individuals have the opportunity to rebuild these connections, whether it's with family, friends, colleagues, or a broader community.

For Clara, a business owner who had struggled with anxiety and substance abuse, recovery brought her closer to her family and friends. She was able to be more present for her children and to nurture her friendships in ways she hadn't been able to before. She also began to build connections with others in the recovery community, finding support and camaraderie in people who truly understood her struggles.

Living sober means building relationships based on authenticity, trust, and mutual support. These connections not only support recovery but also enrich life, providing emotional nourishment and creating a sense of belonging.

Conclusion

Being sober doesn't mean losing your edge—it means gaining clarity, authenticity, and connection. High achievers in recovery can redefine what success looks like, moving away from external validation and toward internal fulfillment. They can become leaders and role models, using their experiences to inspire and guide others. Ultimately, sobriety allows individuals to live fully alive, clear-headed, and connected to the world around them. It opens the door to a life that is richer, more meaningful, and deeply aligned with one's values. By embracing sobriety, high achievers can maintain their ambition while building a more balanced, authentic, and fulfilling life—one that honors both their personal well-being and professional success.

Epilogue

The Power of the Quiet Victory

The path to recovery for high achievers is often paved with quiet victories—small, incremental successes that may go unnoticed by the outside world but are monumental in the journey of personal transformation. It takes immense courage to recover while continuing to perform in high-pressure, high-stakes environments. To face the internal struggles of addiction, burnout, or mental health challenges while maintaining a professional exterior requires not just resilience, but a deep commitment to personal growth and change. High achievers often feel the weight of expectations, not only from others but from themselves. The pressure to "keep up appearances" and "never show weakness" can be suffocating, yet the true victory lies in those quiet moments when the battle is won internally, out of sight of the public eye.

Recovery while performing at your highest level is an extraordinary act of courage. For those who live in the spotlight of their professional achievements, the challenge becomes even more pronounced. Recovery is not a single, grand gesture of success—it's an ongoing process that requires confronting discomfort, admitting vulnerability, and making consistent choices for health over short-term satisfaction. Each time you say "no" to a destructive behavior, each time you choose a healthier coping mechanism, and each time you push through a challenging moment without reverting to old habits, you are winning. These quiet victories—small but powerful—are the foundation upon which long-term recovery and personal success are built.

High achievers often struggle with the concept of imperfection. Society and the professional world demand excellence, and it can be difficult to reconcile the notion of recovery—an inherently imperfect, sometimes messy, process—with the idea of maintaining flawless performance. However, the true measure of success is not found in perfection; it's found in how you rise after setbacks, how you grow from challenges, and how you continue to show up with integrity and authenticity. The quiet victories in recovery aren't about avoiding failure but about navigating it with resilience. They are about taking responsibility for your mistakes, learning from them, and moving forward with a stronger sense of self.

The professional who doesn't just "make it"—but makes it better—embodies this truth. In recovery, success is redefined. It's no longer just about achieving external markers of success—getting the promotion, landing the deal, or winning the award. Instead, it's about achieving a sense of balance, health, and personal alignment that allows for a sustainable version of success. It's about making thoughtful, intentional choices that prioritize well-being without sacrificing ambition. High achievers who recover learn to lead not just through their professional accomplishments but through their growth as individuals. They inspire others by showing that success is not defined by what you've overcome, but by how you continue to evolve.

Recovery doesn't erase your ambitions; it refines them. It challenges you to find purpose beyond the traditional markers of success and to achieve in a way that supports your health and happiness. The professional in recovery is someone who recognizes that true leadership is rooted in vulnerability, self-awareness, and a commitment to creating a sustainable, fulfilling life—not just for themselves, but for those around them. They lead by example, not by perfection, and show that it's possible to excel while staying true to one's values.

As you continue your journey, remember that recovery is not a destination—it's a process, a way of living that you must choose every single day. Along the way, there will be setbacks, moments of doubt, and challenges that may seem insurmountable. However, the quiet victories will always outweigh the loud moments of failure. The courage it takes to recover and perform at the highest level is a testament to your strength, character, and determination.

For those who are on the path of recovery, remember that you are not alone. There are countless resources and support systems available to guide you through your journey. Whether it's therapy, support groups, mindfulness practices, or simply leaning on trusted friends and family, the help you need is out there. And while the journey may be long, it is also incredibly rewarding. You are not just recovering—you are evolving, growing, and becoming a version of yourself that is more aligned with your true potential.

Celebrate the quiet victories. Recognize the power of showing up every day, even when it's hard. And know that the professional who is sober and still sharp is not just someone who has made it—they are someone who is making it better—one step at a time, with courage, integrity, and grace. Keep moving forward, because the best is yet to come.